THE PORTABLE

SCATALOG

CAPTAIN JOHN G. BOURKE,

THIRD CAVALRY, U.S.A.

FELLOW OF THE AMERICAN ASSOCIATION FOR THE
ADVANCEMENT OF SCIENCE;

MEMBER OF THE ANTHROPOLOGICAL SOCIETY, OF WASHINGTON, D.C.;

MEMBER OF THE "CONGRES DES AMERICANISTES;"

ASSOCIATE MEMBER OF THE VICTORIA INSTITUTE AND

PHILOSOPHICAL SOCIETY OF GREAT BRITAIN;

MEMBER OF THE SOCIETY OF AMERICAN FOLK-LORE;

AUTHOR OF

"SNAKE DANCE OF THE MOQUIS OF ARIZONA; "

"AN APACHE CAMPAIGN;"

"NOTES ON THE THEOGONY AND COSMOGONY OF THE MOJAVES;"

"THE GENTILE ORGANIZATION OF THE APACHES;"

"MACKENZIE'S LAST FIGHT WITH THE CHEYENNES,"

AND OTHER WORKS.

THE PORTABLE

SCATALOG

EXCERPTS FROM

SCATALOGIC RITES

of ALL NATIONS

A Dissertation
upon the Employment of Excrementitious Remedial Agents
in Religion, Therapeutics, Divination, Witchcraft, Love-Philters,
etc., in all Parts of the Globe.

BASED UPON ORIGINAL NOTES AND PERSONAL OBSERVATION,
AND UPON COMPILATION FROM OVER ONE THOUSAND AUTHORITIES.

by

JOHN G. BOURKE
1891.

Edited and with an Introduction by
LOUIS P. KAPLAN

Foreword by
SIGMUND FREUD

WILLIAM MORROW AND COMPANY, INC.
NEW YORK

LIBRARY OF CONGRESS CATALOGING-IN-PUBLICATION DATA

Bourke, John Gregory, 1846-1896.
[Scatalogic rites of all nations. Selections]
The portable scatalog: excerpts from Scatalogic Rites of all Nations by John Bourke (1891)/
edited and with an introduction by Louis P. Kaplan: foreword by Sigmund Freud.
p. cm.
Includes index.
ISBN 0-688-13206-5
1. Scatology. I. Kaplan, Louis P. II. Title.
GT3055.B6825 1994 392 dc20 94-6245 CIP

Printed in the United States of America

First Edition

1 2 3 4 5 6 7 8 9 10

BOOK DESIGN BY ALEXANDER BREBNER

FOREWORD

by

SIGMUND FREUD

WHILE I WAS LIVING IN PARIS IN 1885 AS A PUPIL OF Charcot, what chiefly attracted me, apart from the great man's own lectures, were the demonstrations and addresses given by Brouardel. He used to show us from post-mortem material at the morgue how much there was which deserved to be known by doctors but of which science preferred to take no notice. On one occasion he was discussing the indications which enabled one to judge the social rank, character and origin of an unidentified body, and I heard him say: *"Les genoux sales sont le signe d'une fille honnête."* He was using a girl's dirty knees as evidence of her virtue!

The lesson that bodily cleanliness is far more readily associated with vice than with virtue often occurred to me later on, when psycho-analytic work made me acquainted with the way in which civilized men today deal with the problem of their physical nature. They are clearly embarrassed by anything that reminds them too much of their animal origin. They are trying to emulate the 'more perfected angels' in the last scene of *Faust,* who complain:

> *Uns bleibt ein Erdenrest*
> *zu tragen peinlich,*
> *und wär' er von Asbest,*
> *er ist nicht reinlich.*

(For us there remains a trace of the Earth embarrassing to bear; and even if it were out of asbestos, it is not clean.)

Since, however, they must necessarily remain far removed from such perfection, men have chosen to evade the predicament by so far as possible denying the very existence of this inconvenient 'trace of the Earth' by concealing it from one another, and by withholding from it the attention and care which it might claim as an integrating component of their essential being. The wiser course would undoubtedly have been to admit its existence and to dignify it as much as its nature will allow.

It is far from being a simple matter to survey or describe the consequences involved in this way of treating the 'embarrassing trace of the Earth', of which the sexual and excretory functions may be considered the nucleus. It will be enough to mention a single one of these consequences, the one with which we are most concerned here: the fact that science is prohibited from dealing with these proscribed aspects of human life, so that anyone who studies such things is regarded as scarcely less 'improper' than someone who actually *does* improper things.

Nevertheless, psychoanalysis and folklore have not allowed

themselves to be deterred from transgressing these prohibitions and have been able as a result to teach us all kinds of things that are indispensable for an understanding of human nature. If we limit ourselves here to what has been learnt about the excretory functions, it may be said that the chief finding from psycho-analytic research has been the fact that the human infant is obliged to recapitulate during the early part of his development the changes in the attitude of the human race towards excremental matters which probably had their start when *homo sapiens* first raised himself off Mother Earth. In the earliest years of infancy there is as yet no trace of shame about the excretory functions or of disgust at excreta. Small children show great interest in these, just as they do in others of their bodily secretions; they like occupying themselves with them and can derive many kinds of pleasure from doing so. Excreta, regarded as parts of a child's own body and as products of his own organism, have a share in the esteem–the narcissistic esteem, as we should call it–with which he regards everything relating to his self. Children are, indeed, proud of their own excretions and make use of them to help in asserting themselves against adults. Under the influence of its upbringing, the child's coprophilic instincts and inclinations gradually succumb to repression. It learns to keep them secret, to be ashamed of them and to feel disgust at their objects. Strictly speaking, however, the disgust never goes so far as to apply to a child's own excretions, but is content with repudiating them when they are products of other people. The interest which has hitherto been attached to excrement is carried over on to other objects–for instance, from faeces to money, which is, of course, late in acquiring significance for children. Important constituents in the formation of character are developed, or strengthened, from the repression of coprophilic inclinations.

Psychoanalysis further shows that, to begin with, excremental and sexual instincts are not distinct from each other in children. The divorce between them only occurs later and it remains incomplete. Their original affinity, which is established by the anatomy of the human body, still makes itself felt in many ways in normal adults. Finally, it should not be forgotten that these developments can no more be expected to yield a perfect result than any others. Some portion of the old preferences persist, some part of the coprophilic inclinations continue to operate in later life and are expressed in the neuroses, perversions and bad habits of adults.

Folklore has adopted a quite different method of research, and yet it has reached the same results as psychoanalysis. It shows us how incompletely the repression of coprophilic inclinations has been carried out among various peoples at various times and how closely at other cultural levels the treatment of excretory substances approximates to that practised by children. It also demonstrates the persistent and indeed ineradicable nature of coprophilic interests, by displaying to our astonished gaze the multiplicity of applications—in magical ritual, in tribal custom, in observances of religious cults and in the art of healing—by which the old esteem for human excretions has found new expression. The connection, too, with sexual life seems to be fully preserved.

This expansion of our knowledge clearly involves no risk to our

morality. The major part of what is known of the role played by
the excretions in human life has been brought together in J. G.
Bourke's *Scatologic Rites of All Nations*. To make it accessible
. . . is therefore not only a courageous but also a meritorious undertaking.

(1913)

Contents.

Contents 13

Introduction:
Prefatory End Notes
to a Scatalogical Reader
by
Louis P. Kaplan

A LITTLE OVER ONE HUNDRED YEARS AGO, A SMALL PRESS published at private expense a strange volume that was authored by John Gregory Bourke under the comprehensive title of *Scatalogic Rites of All Nations* (Washington, D.C.: Lowdermilk, 1891). The long-winded subtitle focused upon the richness of its contents and its unsuitability for general consumption–"A Dissertation upon the Employment of Excrementitious Remedial Agents in Religion, Therapeutics, Divination, Witchcraft, Love-Philters, etc., in all Parts of the Globe. Based upon Original Notes and Personal Observation, and upon Compilation from over One Thousand Authorities. Not for General Perusal."

But this was only the first life for this curious classic. In 1913, the book was published in translation in Germany in a revised and expanded form under the direction of the folklorist Friedrich Krauss; this edition featured an introduction by the master of the anal stage, Sigmund Freud. The father of psychoanalysis gave his stamp of approval to the scatalog in the following direct manner:

"The major part of what is known of the role played by the ex-cretions in human life has been brought together in J. G. Bourke's *Scatalogic Rites of All Nations*. To make it accessible . . . is therefore not only a courageous but also a meritorious undertaking."

John Bourke (1846–1896) was both a captain in the U.S. Third Cavalry and also an amateur ethnologist who left an overflowing body of written records that detail his version of the conquest of the West in the years after the Civil War. As a soldier and scientist, Bourke was obsessed with how to deal with the problem of re-mains. An aide-de-camp of General George Crook, the soldier assisted in "cleaning up" the remaining territories of the Apaches in the Southwest to make room for white settlement. Meanwhile, Bourke the scientist investigated and collected the remains of this foreign and dying culture. An ethnological approach lies at the core of his trilogy of works—*Scatalogic Rites of All Nations, The Med-icine Men of the Apache,* and *The Snake Dance of the Moquis.* In ad-dition, Bourke was a diarrhetic diarist whose 127 volumes provide a unique autobiographical record of life on the frontier.

The writing of *Scatalogic Rites* may have been inspired by a cul-ture shock that the author experienced while attending a purifi-cation ritual dance among the Zuñi Indians of New Mexico in 1881. Here, Bourke saw how the medicine men of the Nehue-Cue drank vats of urine and fell into ecstasy. Bourke never recov-ered from (nor fully digested) this traumatic experience. Instead, he spent the next decade of his life researching the scatalogical rites, customs, and folklore of all nations. The results of these efforts at "rationalization" and "digestion" constitute *Scatalogic Rites of All Nations.*

It is important to remember that Bourke's scatalog was framed in line with the racist assumptions of an evolutionary model of cultural development and an accompanying belief in the progress of civilization. The evolutionary doctrine held that filthy rites dominated inferior or "primitive" cultures and that such rites in superior or "civilized" societies existed only as survivals of those bygone times. Even while generating more remains himself, Bourke assumed that his scatalog was a contribution to speeding up the extinction of these filthy, primitive rites.

From the fifty-two thematic chapters of Bourke's five-hundred-page compendium of scatalogical lore, I have made a selection of passages, omitting some chapters entirely and others partially. These excerpts do not necessarily follow the original sequential order. Rather, the scatalogical materials have been rearranged for better flow within each chapter. I have also taken the liberty of simplifying Bourke's bulky citational apparatus for the contemporary reader by introducing author and book title before the appropriate quotation.

The reader also should note that Bourke's original oddball orthography has been maintained in *The Portable Scatalog*. The neologistic spelling of *scatalog* and *scatalogical* symbolizes the tension in the book's composition between *catalog* and *scatology*. It records the impossible attempt to provide a comprehensive cataloging of that which remains, that which is left over. Switching back and before between shoveling excrement and collecting knowledge, the scatalog confounds the lowest and highest of values. For that reason, it can be read alternately or simultaneously as an essential document in the library of scatalogical science, and as a classic of toilet humor. Which book is it really? A learned treatise comprising ten years of scientific labors on the scatalogical rites of all nations, or folkloric anecdotes turning the history of civilization into a perverse comedy of excremental manners? It remains with the reader to decide whether to invest in the Bourkean scatalog as library study or as rest room reading, or a combination of the two. That is why, perhaps, the scatalog is now portable.

THE PORTABLE

SCATALOG

1.

THE URINE DANCE

of the

ZUÑIS

N THE EVENING OF NOVEMBER 17, 1881, during my stay in the village of Zuñi, New Mexico, the *Nehue-Cue,* one of the secret orders of the Zuñis, sent word to Mr. Frank H. Cushing, whose guest I was, that they would do us the unusual honor of coming to our house to give us one of their characteristic dances, which, Cushing said, was unprecedented.

The squaws of the governor's family put the long living-room to rights, sweeping the floor and sprinkling it with water to lay the dust. Soon after dark the dancers entered; they were twelve in number, two being boys. The center men were naked, with the exception of black breech-clouts of archaic style. The hair was worn naturally, with a bunch of wild-turkey feathers tied in front, and one of corn husks over each ear. White bands were painted across the face at eyes and mouth. Each wore a collar or neckcloth of black woollen stuff. Broad white bands, one inch wide, were painted around the body at the navel, around the arms, the legs at mid-thighs, and knees. Tortoise-shell rattles hung from the right knee. Blue woollen footless leggings were worn with low-cut moccasins, and in the right hand each waved a wand made of an ear of corn, trimmed with the plumage of the wild turkey and macaw. The others were arrayed in old, cast-off American Army clothing, and all wore white cotton night-caps, with corn-husks twisted into the hair at top of head and ears. Several wore, in addition to the tortoise-shell rattles, strings of brass sleigh-bells at knees. One was more grotesquely attired than the rest, in a long India rubber gossamer "overall," and with a pair of goggles, painted white, over his eyes. His general "get up" was a spirited take-off upon a Mexican priest. Another was a very good counterfeit of a young woman.

To the accompaniment of an oblong drum and of the rattles and bells spoken of, they shuffled into the long room, crammed with spectators of both sexes and of all sizes and ages. Their song was apparently a ludicrous reference to everything and everybody in sight, Cushing and myself receiving special attention, to the uncontrolled merriment of the red-skinned listeners. I had taken my station at one side of the room, seated upon the banquette, and having in front of me a rude bench or table, upon which was a small coal-oil lamp. I suppose that in the halo diffused by the feeble light, and in my "stained-glass attitude," I must have borne some resemblance to the pictures of saints hanging upon the walls of old Mexican churches; to such a fancied resemblance I at least attribute the performance which followed.

The dancers suddenly wheeled into line, threw themselves on

their knees before my table, and with extravagant beatings of breast began an outlandish but faithful mockery of a Mexican Catholic congregation at vespers. One bawled out a parody upon the *paternoster,* another mumbled along in the manner of an old man reciting the rosary, while the fellow with the India-rubber coat jumped up and began a passionate exhortation or sermon, which for mimetic fidelity was incomparable. This kept the audience laughing with sore sides for some moments, until, at a signal from the leader, the dancers suddenly countermarched out of the room in single file as they had entered.

An interlude followed of ten minutes, during which the dusty floor was sprinkled by men who spat water forcibly from their mouths. The *Nehue-Cue* re-entered; this time two of their number were stark naked. Their singing was very peculiar, and sounded like a chorus of chimney-sweeps, and their dance became a stiff-legged jump, with heels kept twelve inches apart. After they had ambled around the room two or three times, Cushing announced in the Zuñi language that a "feast" was ready for them, at which they loudly roared their approbation, and advanced to strike hands with the munificent "Americanos," addressing us in a funny gibberish of broken Spanish, English, and Zuñi. They then squatted upon the ground and consumed with zest large *ollas* full of tea, and dishes of hard tack and sugar. As they were about finishing his squaw entered, carrying an *olla* of urine, of which the filth brute drank heartily.

I refused to believe the evidence of my senses, and asked Cushing if that were really human urine. "Why, certainly," replied he, "and here comes more of it." This time it was a large tin pailful, not less than two gallons. I was standing by the squaw as she offered this strange and abominable refreshment. She made a motion with her hand to indicate to me that it was urine, and one of the old men repeated the Spanish word *mear* (to urinate), while my sense of smell demonstrated the truth of their statements.

The dancers swallowed great draughts, smacked their lips, and, amid the roaring merriment of the spectators, remarked that it was very, very good. The clowns were now upon their mettle, each trying to surpass his neighbors in feats of nastiness. One swallowed a fragment of corn-husk, saying he thought it very good and better than bread; his *vis-à-vis* attempted to chew and gulp down a piece of filthy rag. Another expressed regret that the dance had not been held out of doors, in one of the plazas. There they could show what they could do. There they always made it a point of honor to eat the excrement of men and dogs.

For my own part, I felt satisfied with the omission, particularly as the room, stuffed with one hundred Zuñis, had become so foul and filthy as to be almost unbearable. The dance, as good luck would have it, did not last many minutes, and we soon had a chance to run into the refreshing night air.

To this outline description of a disgusting rite, I have little to add. The Zuñis, in explanation, stated that the *Nehue-Cue* were a Medicine Order, which held these dances from time to time to nure the stomachs of members to any kind of food, no matter ow revolting. The object is said to be to teach fortitude to its members, a well as to teach them the therapeutics of stomachic disorders. In their early history, the Zuñis and other Pueblos suf-fered from constant warfare with savage antagonists and with each other. From the position of their villages, long sieges must have been sustained of necessity, in which famine and disease, no doubt, were the allies counted upon by the invading forces. We may have in this abominable dance a tradition of the extremity to which the Zuñis of long ago were reduced at some unknown period.

Before proceeding further, it may be advisable to clinch the fact that the Urine Dance of the Zuñis was not a sporadic instance, peculiar to that pueblo, or to a particular portion of that pueblo. It was a tribal rite, recognized and commended by the whole community, and entering into the ritual of all the pueblos of the Southwest.

Upon this point, a few words from the author's personal journal of November 24, 1881, may well be introduced to prove its existence among the Moquis–the informant, Nana-je, being a young Moqui of the strictest integrity and veracity: "In the circle, I noticed Nana-je and the young *Nehue-cue* boy who was with us a few nights since. During a pause in the conversation, I asked the young Nehue if he had been drinking any urine lately. This occasioned some laughter among the Indians; but to my surprise Nana-je spoke up and said: 'I am a Nehue also. The Nehue of Zuñi are nothing to the same order among the Moquis. There the Nehue not only drink urine, as you saw done the other night, but also eat human and animal excrement. They eat it here too, but we eat all that is set before us. We have a medicine which makes us drunk like whiskey; we drink a lot of that before we commence; it makes us drunk. We don't care what happens, and nothing of that kind that we eat or drink can ever do us any harm.' The *Nehue-cue* are to be found in all the pueblos on the Rio Grande and close to it; only there they don't do things openly."

Mr. Daniel W. Lord, a gentleman who was for a time associated with Mr. Frank H. Cushing in his investigations among the Zuñis of New Mexico, makes the following statement: "In June, 1888, I was a spectator of an orgy at the Zuñi pueblo in New Mexico. The ceremonial dance of that afternoon had been finished in the small plaza generally used for dances in the northwestern part of the pueblo when this supplementary rite took place. One of the Indians brought into the plaza the excrement to be employed, and it was passed from hand to hand, and eaten. Those taking part in the ceremony were few in number, certainly not more than eight or ten. They drank urine from a large shallow bowl, and meanwhile kept up a running fire of comments and exclamations among themselves, as if urging one another to drink heartily, which indeed they did. At last one of those taking part was made sick, and vomited after the ceremony was over. The inhabitants of the pueblo upon the housetops overlooking the plaza were interested spectators of the scene. Some of the sallies of the actors were received with laughter, and others with signs of disgust and repugnance, but not of disapprobation. The ceremony was not repeated, to my knowledge, during my stay at the pueblo, which continued till July, 1889."

2.

THE FEAST

of

FOOLS

in

EUROPE

LOSELY CORRESPONDING TO THIS URINE DANCE of the Zuñis was the Feast of Fools in Continental Europe, the description of which here given is quoted from Jacques Dulaure's *Des Divinités Génératrices (Of the Generative Gods)*:

"The high mass then commenced. All the clerics participated, and they either wore a blackened countenance or covered themselves with hideous and ridiculous masks. During the celebration, a few, who were dressed up as clowns or women, danced in the middle of the choir and sang silly and obscene songs. The others ate sausages and blood-puddings (*boudin*) upon the altar, played cards or dice in front of the priest celebrating mass, put stinking stuff from the leather of old shoes in the censer and made them inhale this incense.

After the mass, there were new acts of extravagance and impiety. The priests, mixed up with the garments of both sexes, ran around, danced in the church, stimulated all sorts of foolishness, provoked all sorts of licentious actions that a boundless imagination inspired in them. There was no more restraint and no more modesty. No dam could stop the tide of madness and passion.

In the middle of the tumult, the blasphemy, and the undisciplined songs, one noticed a few who threw away all their clothes entirely, and others who gave themselves over to the most indecent libertinage.

Mounted on dung-carts, the actors amused themselves by throwing ordure upon the crowd that surrounded them. These scenes were always accompanied by impious and scatalogical songs."

Let us compare the Feast of Fools and the Urine Dance. In the above description may be seen that the principal actors (taking possession of the church during high mass) had their faces daubed and painted, or masked in a harlequin manner; that they were dressed as clowns or as women; that they ate upon the altar itself sausages and blood-puddings. Now the word "blood-pudding" in French is *boudin,* but *boudin* also meant "excrement." Add to this the feature that these clowns, after leaving the church, took their stand in dung-carts (*tombereaux*), and threw *ordure* upon the bystanders; and finally that some of these actors appeared perfectly naked, and it must be admitted that there is certainly a wonderful concatenation of resemblances between these filthy and inexplicable rites on different sides of a great ocean.

Dulaure makes no attempt to trace the origin of these ceremonies in France. He contents himself with saying, "These ceremonies have lasted for twelve or fifteen centuries," or, in other words, that they were of Pagan origin. In twelve or fifteen hundred years the rite might have been well sublimed from the eating of pure excrement, as among the Zuñis, to the consumption of the *boudin*, the excrement symbol. Conceding for the moment that this suspicion is correct, we have a proof of the antiquity of the urine dance among the Zuñis.

Reverend Thomas Fosbroke gives his version in the *Cyclopaedia of Antiquities*: "In the Feast of Fools they put on masks, took the dress of women, and danced and sung in the choir, ate fat cakes upon the horn of the altar, where the celebrating priest played at dice, put stinking stuff from the leather of old shoes in the censer, jumped about the church, with the addition of obscene jests, songs, and unseemly attitudes. Another part of this indecorous buffoonery was shaving the precentor of fools upon a stage erected before the church in the presence of the people; and during the operation he amused them with lewd and vulgar discourses and gestures. They also had carts full of ordure which they threw occasionally upon the populace. This exhibition was always at Christmas time or near it, but was not confined to a particular day."

This reference to the use of the pudding or sausage on the altar itself is the most persistent feature in the descriptions of the whole ceremony. But little difficulty will be experienced in showing that it was originally an excrement sausage, prepared and offered up, perhaps eaten, for a definite purpose. This phase of the subject will be considered further on; for the present only one citation need be introduced to show that in carnival time human excrement itself, and not the symbol, made its appearance.

This citation comes from John Brand's *Popular Antiquities*: "The following extract from Barnaby Googe's translation of *Naogeorgus* will show the extent of these festivities (i.e., those of the carnival at Shrove Tuesday). After describing the wanton behavior of men dressed as women and of women arrayed in the garb of men, of clowns dressed as devils, as animals, or running about perfectly naked, the account goes on to say:

> *But others bear a torde, that on a cushion soft they lay;*
> *And one there is that with a flap doth keep the flies away:*
> *I would there might another be, an officer of those,*
> *Whose room might serve to take away the scent from every nose."*

The authors who have referred at greater or less length, and with more or less preciseness, to the Feast of Fools, Feast of Asses, and others of that kind, are legion. Unfortunately, without an exception, they have contented themselves with a description of the obscene absurdities connected with these popular religious gatherings, without attempting an analysis of the underlying motives which prompted them, or even making an intelligent effort to trace their origin. Where the last has been alluded to at all, it has almost invariably been with the assertion that the Feast of Fools was a survival from the Roman Saturnalia.

This can scarcely have been the case. In the progress of this work it is purposed to make evident that the use of human and animal egestae in religious ceremonial was common all over the world, antedating the Roman Saturnalia, or at least totally unconnected with it. The correct interpretation of the Feast of Fools would, therefore, seem to be that which recognized it as a reversion to a pre-Christian type of thought dating back to the earliest appearance of the Aryan race in Europe.

3.

HUMAN EXCREMENT
USED IN FOOD
by the
INSANE AND OTHERS

HE SUBJECT OF EXCREMENT-EATING AMONG insane persons has engaged the attention of medical experts. H. B. Obersteiner, in a communication to the *Psychiatrisches Centralblatt* (Vienna, 1871), informs that periodical that Dr. A. Erlenmeyer, Jr., induced by a lecture delivered by Professor Lang in 1872, had prepared a tabulated series of data embodying the results of his observations upon the existence of coprophagy among insane persons. He found that one in a hundred persons suffering from mental diseases indulged in this abnormal appetite. The majority of these were men. No particular relation could be established between excrement-eating and Onanism; and no deleterious effect upon the alimentary organs was detected.

"A boy of four years old had fouled in bed; but being much afraid of whipping, he ate his own dung, yet he could not blot the sign out of the sheets; wherefore, being asked by threatenings, he at length tells the chance. But being asked of its savor, he said it was of a stinking and somewhat sweet one. A noble little virgin, being very desirous of her salvation, eats her own dung, and was weak and sick. She was asked of what savor it was, and she answered it was of a stinking and a waterishly sweet one." In his *Oritrika,* Jean Baptiste Von Helmont says that these examples were personally known to him, as was that of the painter of Brussels who, going mad, subsisted for twenty-three days on his own excrements.

A French lady was in the habit of carrying about her pulverized human excrements, which she ate, and would afterwards lick her fingers. In addition, Christian Franz Paullini gives the instance of the painter of Brussels already cited on the preceding page in *Dreck Apothek (Filth Pharmacy).*

According to the *Bibliotheca Scatologica,* "Bouillon Lagrange, Parisian pharmacist, who was referred to as Bouillon *à Pointu* (the Sharp-Pointed) by his colleagues, published a book entitled *La Chimie du Gout (The Chemistry of Taste)* which deals with the fabrication of table liquors. He gives the recipe for a preparation that he calls *Eau de Mille Fleurs* which is composed of cow dung distilled in table water." Angelo De Gubernatis comments in *Zoological Mythology*: "As to the excrements of the cow, they are still used to form the so-called *eau de mille fleurs* recommended by several pharmacopoeias as a remedy for cachexy."

Bibliotheca Scatologica continues: "In Paris, there was a rich citizen named Paperal who had a strange taste for the excrement of small children. The story even relates that he always ate it with a golden spoon. This is not the only example of such a bizarre taste. Bouillon always carried around a golden box with him which was never filled with tobacco, but rather with human excrement."

The following appeared in an article headed "The Last Cholera Epidemic in Paris" in the *General Homœopathic Journal* (1886): "The neighbors of an establishment famous for its excellent bread, pastry, and similar products of luxury, complained again and again of the disgusting smells which prevailed therein and which penetrated into their dwellings. The appearance of cholera finally lent force to these complaints, and the sanitary inspectors who were sent to investigate the matter found that there was a connection between the water-closets of these dwellings and the reservoir containing the water used in the preparation of the bread. Chemists have evidently no difficulty in demonstrating that water impregnated with 'extract of water-closet' has the peculiar property of causing dough to rise particularly fine, thereby imparting to bread the nice appearance and pleasant flavor which is the principal quality of luxurious bread."

A case is given in Martin Schurig's *Chylologia* of a patient who, having once experienced the beneficial effects of mouse-dung in some complaint, became a confirmed mouse-dung eater, and was in the habit of picking up from the floor of his house before the servants could sweep it away. Meanwhile, Paullini confirms that the *enceinte* wife of a farmer in the town of Hassfort on the Main ate the excrements of her husband, warm and smoking.

An extract is here given from a letter sent to Charlotte Elizabeth of Bavaria, Princess-Palatine, daughter of Charles Louis, Elector-Palatine of the Rhine, born at Heidelberg, in 1652. She married the brother of Louis XIV, the widower of Henrietta Maria of

England. The letter in question was sent her by her aunt, the wife of the Elector of Hanover, and may serve to give an idea of the boldness of the opinions entertained by the ladies of high rank in that era, and the coarseness with which they expressed them:

Hannover, October 31, 1694

If meat makes shit, it is also right to say that shit makes meat. Is it not so that even at the finest tables shit is served as ragout? Bratwurst, chitterlings, blood sausages—what are they but different kinds of ragout served in shit sacks!

4.

The Employment of Excrement

in

Food

by

Savage Tribes

HE VERY EARLIEST ACCOUNTS OF THE INDIANS of Florida and Texas refer to the use of such aliment. Cabeza de Vaca, one of the survivors of the ill-fated expedition of Panfilo de Narvaez, was a prisoner among various tribes for many years, and finally, accompanied by three comrades as wretched as himself, succeeded in traversing the continent, coming out at Culiacan, on the Pacific Coast, in 1536. His narrative says that the Floridians "for food, dug roots, and that they ate spiders, ants' eggs, worms, lizards, salamanders, snakes, earth, wood, the dung of deer, and many other things." The same account, given in Samuel Purchas' *Pilgrims,* expresses it that "they also eat earth, wood, and whatever they can get; the dung of wild beasts." These remarks may be understood as applying to all tribes seen by this early explorer east of the Rocky Mountains.

In *Historia de las Indias,* Gomara identifies this loathsome diet with a particular tribe, the Yaguaces of Florida. "They eat spiders, ants, worms, lizards of two kinds, snakes, earth, wood, and ordure of all kinds of wild animals."

The California Indians were still viler. The German Jesuit, Father Jacob Baegert, speaking of the Lower Californians (among whom he resided continuously from 1748 to 1765), says: "They eat the seeds of the *pitahaya* (giant catus) which have passed off undigested from their own stomachs. They gather their own excrement, separate the seeds from it, roast, grind, and eat them, making merry over the loathsome meal." And again: "In the mission of Saint Ignatius, there are persons who will attach a piece of meat to a string and swallow it and pull it out again a dozen times in succession, for the sake of protracting the enjoyment of its taste."

A similar use of meat tied to a string is understood to have once been practiced by European sailors for the purpose of teasing green comrades suffering from the agonies of sea-sickness.

The same information is to be found in François Clavigero's *Historia de la Baja California* and in H. H. Bancroft's *Native Races of the Pacific Slope*. Both derive their information from Father Baegert. Orozco y Berra also has the story, but he adds that oftentimes numbers of the Californians would meet and pass the delicious tidbit from mouth to mouth.

Castañeda alludes to the Californians as a race of naked savages, who ate their own excrement.

The Indians of North America, according to Daniel Harmon, "boil the buffalo paunch with much of its dung adhering to it"—a filthy mode of cooking which in itself would mean little, since it can be paralleled in almost all tribes. But in another paragraph of his *Journal,* the same author says: "Many consider a broth made by means of the dung of the caribou and the hare to be a dainty dish."

In *Deserts,* the Abbé Domenech asserts the same of the bands near Lake Superior: "In boiling their wild rice to eat, they mix it with the excrement of rabbits—a delicacy appreciated by the epicures among them."

According to Purchas, the Mosagueys make themselves a "pottage with milk and fresh dung of kine, which, mixed together and heated at the fire, they drinke, saying it makes them strong."

In Beveridge's *The Aborigines of Victoria and Riverina,* one learns that the savages of Australia "make a sweet and luscious beverage by mixing *taarp* with water. *Taarp* is the excrement of a small green beetle, wherein the larvae thereof are deposited."

According to Élie Réclus in *Les Primitifs,* "The Ygarrotes of the Philipines sprinkle the liquidous excrement of a freshly slaughtered buffalo over their raw fish as a sauce."

In *Travels to Discover the Source of the Nile,* James Bruce reports: "The water of Dobelew and Irwee tasted strongly of musk, from the dung of the goats and antelopes, and the smell before you drink it is more nauseous than the taste."

From thus enduring water polluted with the excrements of animals to drinking beverages to which urine has been purposely added, as Sir Samuel Baker and Colonel Chaille Long show to have been the custom of the Negroes near Gondokoro with their milk, is but a very small step.

Chaille Long relates that in Central Africa he and his men were obliged to drink water which was a mixture of the excrements of the rhinoceros and the elephant.

The tribes of Angola, West Africa, cook the entrails of deer without removing the contents. This is for the purpose of getting a flavor, as the excrement itself is not eaten.

The Aleuts and Indians from the extreme northern coast of America with George Melville's party displayed an appetite for the half-digested contents of the paunches of the seals killed by them. This appetite was not due to lack of food, as Chief Engineer Melville, U.S. Navy, takes care to explain. At another time he detected his "natives" in the act of eating "plentifully, though covertly, of the droppings of the reindeer."

Peter Kolbein states in *Voyage to the Cape of Good Hope,* "Some authors have said that all the Hottentots devour the entrails of beasts, uncleansed of their filth and excrements and that, whether sound or rotten, they consider them as the greatest delicacies in the world; but this is not true. I have always found that when they had entrails to eat they turned and stripped them of their filth and washed them in clear water."

5.

The Ordure
of
the Grand Lama
of
Thibet

Rosinus Lentilius, in the *Ephemeridum Physico-Medicorum* (Leipzig, 1694), speaks of the Grand Lama of Thibet as held in such high veneration by the devotees of his faith that his excrements, carefully collected, dried, powdered, and sold at high prices by the priests, were used as a sternutatory powder, to induce sneezing, as a condiment for their food, and as a remedy for all the graver forms of disease.

Konrad Maltebrun's *Universal Geography* asserts it in positive terms: "It is a certain fact that the refuse excreted from his body is collected with sacred solicitude, to be employed as amulets and infallible antidotes to disease." Jean-Baptiste Tavernier, whose opportunities for observation were excellent, asserted the fact without ambiguity. The excrement of the Grand Lama was carefully collected, dried, and in various ways used as a condiment, as a snuff, and as a medicine.

A Description of Thibet has the following: "There is no king in the world more feared and respected by his subjects than the king of Butan; being in a manner adored by them. The merchants assured Tavernier that those about the king preserve his ordure, dry it, and reduce it to a powder like snuff; that then putting it into boxes, they go every market-day and present it to the chief traders and farmers, who recompensing them for their great kindness, carry it home as a great rarity, and when they feast their friends, strew it upon their meat. The author adds that two of them showed him their boxes with the powder in them."

It continues, "Grueber assures us that the grandees of the kingdom are very anxious to procure the excrements of this divinity (i.e., the Grand Lama), which they usually wear about their necks as relics. In another place he says that the Lamas make a great advantage by the large presents they receive for helping the grandees to some of his excrements, or urine; for, by wearing the first about their necks, and mixing the latter with their victuals, they imagine themselves to be secure against all bodily infirmities. In confirmation of this, Gerbillon informs us that the Mongols wear his excrements, pulverized, in little bags about their necks, as precious relics, capable of preserving them from all misfortunes, and curing them of all sorts of distempers. When this Jesuit was on his second journey into Western Tartary, a deputy from one of the principal lamas offered the emperor's uncle a certain powder, contained in a little packet of very white paper, neatly wrapped up in a scarf of a very white taffety; but that prince told him that as it was not the custom of the Manchews to make use of such things, he durst not receive it. The author took this powder to be either some of the Great Lama's excrements, or the ashes of something that had been used by him."

In "Memorandum on Thibet," Warren Hastings speaks of the Thibetan priests of high degree, the *Ku-tchuck-tus,* who, he says, "admit a superiority in the Dalai Lama, so that his excrements are sold as charms, at great price, among all the Tartar tribes of this religion."

The Reverend James Gilmour writes in *Among the Mongols:* "When famous lamas die and their bodies are burnt, little white pills are reported as found among the ashes, and sold for large sums to the devout, as being the concentrated virtue of the man and possessing the power of insuring a happy future for him who swallows one near death. This is quite common. I heard of one man who improved on this by giving out that these little pills were in the habit of coming out through the skin of various parts of the body. These pills, called *Sharil,* met with a ready sale, and then the man himself reaped the reward of his virtue and did not allow all the profit to go to his heir."

This writer says that these sacred pills are white; another one describes them as black, while those obtained by the author from Mr. W. W. Rockhill are red.

The following is from a manuscript by Rockhill, entitled "The Lamaist Ceremony called the Making of the Mani Pills":

"Certain indestructible particles of the bodies of the Buddhas and saints, as well as certain other bodily remains, have ever been considered by Buddhists to enjoy certain properties, such as that of emitting light, and of having great curative properties. The travels of Huein-Tsang and of Fa-lisien are filled with accounts of the discovery of such treasures, and of the supernatural properties which they possessed. Among Thibetans, the first class of these relics is known as *pedung,* the second as *dung-rus.* They say the *pedung* are minute globules found in the bones of Buddhas and saints, that they possess a wonderful brilliancy, and that sometimes they may be seen on the exterior of some saintly person, when they have the appearance of brilliant drops of sweat. While these *pedung* have most potent curative properties, they become also the palladium of the locality fortunate enough to have them. By a natural extension of the idea of the power of *pedung,* Thibetans have come to think that if one preserves and carries about on one's person even a little of the excretions, or of the hair or nail-trimmings of a saint who is known to have *pedung,* such, for instance, as the Dalai Lama, or the Panchen Rimpoche, they will shield him from gun or sword wounds, sickness, etc.; hence the extraordinary objects one so often finds in Thibetan charm-boxes (*Ka Wo*)."

Mr. Rockhill explains that the word *pedung* used in the above description, means "remains." Taking into consideration the fact that these people, although remotely, are related to the Aryan stock, which is the ancestor of the English, German, Irish, Latin, and others, from which we spring, the meaning, as here given, is certainly not without significance. "Dung," in our own tongue, means nothing more nor less than remains, reliquiae of a certain kind.

Webster traces the word "dung" to the Anglo-Saxon *dung, dyncg, dincg*—excrement; *Dyngan,* to dung; New High German, *dung, dunger;* Old High German, *Tunga;* Swedish *Dynga;* Danish,

Dynge and *Dyngd*; Icelandic, *Dyngia* and *Dy*. This shows it to be essentially Indo-Germanic in type, and fairly to be compared with the words *"pedung"* and *"dung-rus"* of Mr. Rockhill's manuscript.

In the country of Ur of the Chaldees, which was the home of Abraham (Genesis, XI, 2), there reigned a king, "the father of Dungi." The exact meaning of the name "Dungi" has not been made known. The name of the king himself, strangely enough, was Urea or Uri—it is read both ways. His date has been fixed at 3,000 years B.C.

The information in the preceding paragraph was furnished by Professor Otis T. Mason of the National Museum, Washington, D.C.

The sacred pills presented by Rockhill to the author were enclosed in a silver reliquary, elaborately ornamented. In size, they were about as large as quail shot. Their color was almost orange, or between that and an ochreous red.

Through the kindness of Surgeon-General John Moore (U.S. Army), they were analyzed by Dr. Mew (U.S. Army) with the following results:

> *April 18, 1889*
>
> *I have at length found time to examine the Grand Lama's ordure, and write to say that I find nothing at all remarkable in it. He had been feeding on a farinaceous diet, for I found by the microscope a large amount of undigested starch in the field, the presence of which I verified by the usual iodine test, which gave an abundant reaction.*
>
> *There was also present much cellulose, or what appeared to be cellulose, from which I infer that the flour used (which was not of wheat) was of a coarse quality, and probably not made in Minnesota.*

A slight reaction for biliary matter seemed to show that there was no obstruction of the bile ducts. These tests about used up the four very small pills of the Lama's ordure.

   Very respectfully and sincerely yours,

                                        (Signed) W. M. Mew

Such use of the excrement of ecclesiastical dignitaries was also indicated in Oriental literature. In the *Arabian Nights,* King Afrida says to the Emirs, among other things, " 'And I purpose this night to sacre you all with the Holy Incense.' " When the Emirs heard these words, they kissed the ground before him. Now the incense which he designated was the excrement of the Chief Patriarch, the denier, the defiler of the truth, and they sought for it with such instance, and they so highly valued it, that the high-priests of the Greeks used to send it to all the countries of the Christians in silken wraps, after mixing it with musk and ambergris. Hearing of it, kings would pay a thousand gold pieces for every dram, and they sent for and sought it to fumigate brides withal. And the Chief Priests and the Great Kings were wont to use a little of it as a collyrium (salve) for the eyes, and as a remedy in sickness and colic. And the Patriarchs used to mix their own skite (excrement) with it, for that the skite of the Chief Patriarch would not suffice for ten countries." In Richard Burton's Index, this is called "Holy Merde."

6.

THE STERCORANISTES

*T*HAT CHRISTIAN POLEMICS HAVE NOT BEEN entirely free from such ideas may be shown satisfactorily to any one having the leisure to examine the various phases of the discussion upon the doctrine of the Eucharist.

The word *stercoranistes,* or *stercorarians,* is not to be found in the last edition of the *Encyclopaedia Britannica.* But in the edition of 1841, the definition of the word is as follows: "Stercorarians, or Stercoranistes, formed from *stercus,* 'dung,' a name which those of the Romish church originally gave to such as held that the host was liable to digestion and all its consequences, like other food." This definition was copied verbatim in Rees' *Cyclopaedia of Arts, Sciences, and Literature.*

The dispute upon *Stercoranisme* began in 831 upon the appearance of a theological treatise by a monk named Paschasius Radbert.

According to John Lawrence von Mosheim's *Institutes of Eccle-*

siastical History, "The grossly sensual conception of the presence of the Lord's body in the sacrament, according to which that body is eaten, digested, and evacuated like ordinary food, is of ancient standing, though not found in Origen, nor perhaps in Rhabanus Maurus. It certainly originated with a class of false teachers contemporary with or earlier than Rhabanus Maurus, whom Paschasius Radbert condemns. Radbert argued, 'It is therefore a sacrilege to hold that in this mystery the host would be transformed into excrement like in the digestion of other foods.' He does not, however, apply the term *Stercoranistes* to his opponents. Cardinal Humbert is the first to so employ the word. This use was in a polemic against Nicetas Pectoratus, written in support of Azymitism. From this source the word was adopted into common usage."

Brand, in his *Encyclopaedia of Science, Literature, and Art* article "Stercoranism," says: "A nickname which seems to have been applied in the Western churches in the fifth and sixth centuries to those who held the opinion that a change took place in the consecrated elements, so as to render the divine body subject to the act of digestion." He refers to Mosheim's *Ecclesiastical History* for a fuller account.

The *First Gospel of the Infancy of Jesus Christ* seems to have been received by the Gnostics of the second century as canonical, and accepted in the same sense of Eusebius, Athanasius, Chrysostom, and others of the Fathers and writers of the Church. Sozomen was told by travellers in Egypt that they had heard in that country of the miracles performed by the water in which the infant Jesus had been washed. According to Ahmed ben Idris, this gospel was used in parts of the East in common with the other gospels; while

Ocobius de Castro asserts that in many churches of Asia and Africa it was recited exclusively. But, on the other hand, all the apocrypha were condemned by Pope Gelasius in the fifth century; and this interdict was not repealed until the time of Paul IV in the sixteenth century.

In the following extracts it will noted that the miracles recorded were wrought either by the swaddling clothes themselves or by the water in which they had been cleansed; and the inference is that the excreta of Christ were believed, as in many other instances, to have the character of a panacea, as well as generally miraculous properties.

The Madonna gave one of the swaddling clothes of Christ to the Wise Men of the East who visited him. They took it home, "and having, according to the custom of their country, made a fire, they worshipped it. And casting the swaddling cloth into the fire, the fire took it and kept it" (1 Infancy III, 6–7).

On arrival in Egypt after the Flight–"When the Lady Saint Mary had washed the swaddling clothes of the Lord Christ and hanged them out to dry upon a post, a certain boy possessed with the devil took down one of them and put it upon his head. And presently the devils began to come out of his mouth and fly away in the shape of crows and serpents. And from this time the boy was healed by the power of the Lord Christ" (1 Inf. IV, 15–17).

"On the return journey from Egypt, Christ had healed by a kiss a lady whom cursed Satan had leaped upon in the form of a serpent. On the morrow, the same woman brought perfumed water to wash the Lord Jesus; when she had washed him, she preserved the water. And there was a girl whose body was white with leprosy, who being sprinkled with this water was instantly cleansed from her leprosy" (1 Inf. VI, 16–17).

There is another example of exactly the same kind. "And in Matarea the Lord Jesus caused a well to spring forth, in which Saint Mary washed his coat. And a balsam is produced or grown in that country from the sweat which ran down there from the Lord Jesus" (1 Inf. VIII).

The subjoined extract is from *Mélusine* edited by Henri Gaidoz in Paris on May 5, 1888.

"In connection with the daily relics of the Dalai-Lama out of which one makes pills for the devout, there comes a story brought to our attention by John Stokes about a curious reference in the annals of Irish history that the publisher of this review would not want to 'hold back.' We feel that this reference is interesting enough to translate here. This 'act of faith' took place in the year 605 A.D., and the hero of the tale is King Aedh who had the surname Uairidhnach.

One day during the time when he was still only the crown prince, Aedh went through the territory of Othain-Muira. He washed his hands in a brook which passed through the region of this town. He also took water in order to wash his face. But one of his people stopped him. 'My Lord,' he said to him, 'do not put this water on your face!' 'And why not?' asked the King. 'I am ashamed to tell you,' he replied. 'How can you be ashamed to speak the truth?' asked the King. 'Alright then,' he said, 'the thing is this. Above this body of water, one finds the water-closet of the clergymen.' 'And does the chief cleric himself come here in order to relieve himself?'

'Yes, he comes here himself,' answered the Page. 'I will not only put this water on my face,' said the King, 'but I will also put it in my mouth and I will drink from it.' (And he truly drank three mouthfuls of it.) He explained this action as follows: 'Because the water in which such a man relieves himself is as good as the Eucharist as far as I am concerned.'

This was recounted to Muira (the chief cleric), and he thanked God that Aedh had such faith; and he called Aedh unto him and said to him: 'Dear son, as a reward for the respect that you have shown to the Church, I promise you in the presence of God that you will soon obtain the crown of Ireland, that you will be victorious and triumph over your enemies, that you will not die a sudden death, that you will receive the body of Christ from my hand, and that I will pray for you to the Lord so that you will live to be an old man when the Lord takes you from this life.'

And it was a short time hereafter that Aedh really did obtain the crown of Ireland, and he gave fertile lands to Muira of Othain.

As the reader cannot fail to note, it is for edification that the annalist, a clergyman himself, recounts this story. In effect, it honors the piety of the king and it proves that 'the respect accorded the Church has received its reward.' In essence, what comes from men of God partakes of the sacred character of the God whom they represent.

If one would try to expand this examination of hieratic scatology further, one would doubtlessly find many beliefs and practices that are repugnant to our civilized tastes. Nevertheless, they are quite reasonable in a certain sense if one accepts their point of departure, if one does not condemn their logic, and, above all, if one recalls that the disgust for the remains of the digestion has become an inhibition only on account of civilized life and social habits. People who do not wash their hands surely smell quite differently than we do, and perhaps they do not smell at all. In any case, our ancestors from the age of the cavemen had a less developed sense of smell. One ascertains that the shamans of the Namas (a Hottentot tribe) celebrate their marriages by urinating on the newlyweds. This is a substitute for our holy water. The shaman is in fact 'a man of God' in a very special sense because, when he abandons himself to the wild dances that are a part of the cult, they believe that the God has descended upon him, not spiritually, but physically."

The next paragraph is taken from the work of the missionary Turner, who lived for seventeen years in the islands of Polynesia. They appear in his book *Samoa.* "Here is the place to recall a linguistic custom of the inhabitants of Samoa in Polynesia. When a woman is on the verge of giving birth, they address a prayer to the God or protective spirit of the father's family and that of the mother's family. When the infant is born, the mother asks to which God they were in the process of praying at that very moment. They take note of this very carefully, and this God will become the protective spirit of the child throughout his life. Out of respect for this God, one calls the child his 'excrement.' During his childhood one really does refer to him in this manner, as with a nickname, as the 'excrement of Tongo' or 'excrement of Satia' or some other God, as the case might be. This formulation is indeed crude, but, in any event, the intention comes from a feeling of respect and piety in relation to the divinity in a completely materialist guise."

7.

POISONOUS MUSHROOMS USED

in

UR-ORGIES

HE POISONOUS FUNGUS *AMANITA MUSCARIA* possesses an intoxicating property, and is employed by Northern nations as an inebriant. The following is the account of Georg Langsdorff, as given by Greville in the *English Cyclopaedia* of 1854:

"This variety of *Amanita muscaria* is used by the inhabitants of the northeastern parts of Asia in the same manner as wine, brandy, arrack, opium, etc. is by other nations. Such fungi are found most plentifully about Wischna, Kamtchatka, and Willowa Derecona, and are very abundant in some seasons, and scarce in others. They are collected in the hottest months, and hung up by a string to dry in the air; some dry themselves on the ground, and are said to be far more narcotic than those artificially preserved. Small, deep-colored specimens, deeply covered with warts, are also said to be more powerful than those of a larger sizer and paler color.

The usual mode of taking the fungus is to roll it up like a bolus and swallow it without chewing, which the Kamtchkadales say would disorder the stomach.

The desired effect comes in from one to two hours after taking the fungus. Giddiness and drunkenness result in the same manner as from wine or spirits. Cheerful emotions of the mind are first produced, the countenance becomes flushed, involuntary words and actions follow, and sometimes at last an entire loss of consciousness. It renders some remarkably active, and proves highly stimulating to muscular exertion. By too large a dose, violent spasmodic effects are produced. So very exciting to the nervous system in some individuals is this fungus that the effects are often very ludicrous. If a person under its influence wishes to step over a straw or small stick, he takes a stride or a jump sufficient to clear the trunk of a tree. A talkative person cannot keep silence or secrets, and one fond of music is perpetually singing.

The most singular effect of the *Amanita* is the influence it possesses over the urine. It is said that from time immemorial the inhabitants have known that the fungus imparts an intoxicating quality to that secretion, which continues for a considerable time after taking it. For instance, a man moderately intoxicated today will by the next morning have slept himself sober; but (as is the custom) by taking a cup of his urine he will be more powerfully intoxicated than he was the preceding day. It is therefore not uncommon for confirmed drunkards to preserve their urine as a precious liquor against a scarcity of the fungus.

The intoxicating property of the urine is capable of being propagated, for every one who partakes of it has his urine similarly affected. Thus, with a very few *Amanitae,* a party of drunkards may keep up their debauch for a week. Dr. Langsdorff mentions that by means of the second person taking the urine of the first, the third of the second, and so on, intoxication may be propagated through five individuals."

In *Letters from a Citizen of the World,* Oliver Goldsmith speaks of "a curious custom" among "the Tartars of Koraki. The Russians who trade with them carry thither a kind of mushroom. These mushrooms the rich Tartars lay up in large quantities for the winter; and when a nobleman makes a mushroom feast all the neighbors around are invited. The mushrooms are prepared by boiling, by which the water acquires an intoxicating quality, and is a sort of drink which the Tartars prize beyond all other. When the nobility and the ladies are assembled, and the ceremonies usual between people of distinction over, the mushroom broth goes freely round, and they laugh, talk *double-entendres,* grow fuddled, and become excellent company. The poorer sort, who love mushroom broth to distraction as well as the rich, but cannot afford it at first hand, post themselves on these occasions round the huts of the rich, and watch the opportunity of the ladies and gentlemen as they come down to pass the liquor, and holding a wooden bowl, catch the delicious fluid, very little altered by filtration, being still strongly tinctured with the intoxicating quality. Of this they drink with the utmost satisfaction, and thus they get as drunk and as jovial as their betters.

'Happy nobility!' cried my companion, 'who can fear no diminution of respect unless seized with strangury, and who when drunk are most useful! Though we have not this custom among us, I foresee that if it were introduced, we might have many a toad-eater in England ready to drink from the wooden bowl on these occasions, and to praise the flavor of his lordship's liquor. As we have different classes of gentry, who knows but we may see a lord holding the bowl to the minister, a knight holding it to his lordship, and a simple squire drinking it double distilled from the loins of knighthood?' "

Dr. James Grieve reports on the effects of the fungus in *The History of Kamtchatka and the Kurile Islands*: "It is observed whenever they have eaten of this plant, they maintain that whatever foolish things they did, they only obeyed the commands of the mushroom; however, the use of it is so dangerous that unless they were well looked after, it would be the destruction of numbers of them. The Kamtchadales do not much care to relate these drunken frolics, and perhaps the continual use of it renders it less dangerous to them. One of our Cossacks resolved to eat of this mushroom in order to surprise his comrades, and this he actually did; but it was with great difficulty they preserved his life. Another of the inhabitants of Kamtchatka, by the use of this mushroom, imagined that he was upon the brink of hell ready to be thrown in, and that the mushroom ordered him to fall on his knees and make a full confession of all the sins he could remember, which he did before a great number of his comrades, to their no small diversion. It is related that a soldier of the garrison, having eaten a little of this mushroom, walked a great way without any fatigue; but at last, having taken too great a quantity, he died. My interpreter drank some of this juice without knowing of it, and became so mad that it was with difficulty we kept him from ripping open his belly, being, as he said, ordered to do so by the mushroom."

Surgeon B. J. D. Irwin (U.S. Army) writes in a personal letter: "Captain Healey, of the revenue cutter *Bear,* brought to this place, last autumn, a shipwrecked seaman, who had been rescued by the Siberian Tchuktchis, with whom he remained some two years. He described their mode of making an intoxicating liquor thus: in the summer, mushrooms or fungi were collected in large quantity, and eaten by a man who, like our Indians, prepared himself by fasting for the feast. After eating enormous quantities of the fungi, he vomited into a receptacle, and again loaded up, time and again, and disgorged the stuff in a semi-fermented or half-digested condition. It was swallowed by those who were waiting for the drink; and his urine was also imbibed, to aid in producing a debauch, resulting in frenzied intoxication."

Meanwhile Captain M. A. Healey provides his account: "The seaman J. B. Vincent, whom I found with the Tchuktchi last summer, says that they collect in their tents a species of fungi, and during their carnival season, corresponding to about our Christmas holidays, one man is selected, who masticates a quantity of it, and drinks an enormous supply of water; he then gets into his deer's team, and is driven from camp to camp, repeating the mastication and drinking at each camp, where his urine is drunk by the people with an effect of intoxication. The arrival of this man is hailed with much pomp and ceremony by the people. The seaman, Vincent, witnessed several of these ceremonies, and was pressed to join in the orgies, being called 'a boy,' when he declined to sustain his part."

If not for Sacred Intoxication, then the question may be asked: For what reason did the Siberians and others use the poisonous fungus? The only answer possible is, that, in the absence of cereals and under the pressure of a desire for stimulants, the aborigines resorted to all kinds of vegetable substances, as can be shown to have been the case from the history of many nations. Mythology is replete with examples of the occult virtues of plants, such as the mandrake and many others.

Certainly, the religious veneration with which they were regarded was not more fully deserved than by this wonderful toxic— the *Amanita muscaria*. The thirst for stimulants has been very generally diffused all over the world; there is no reason to believe that any tribe has existed without an occasional use of something of the kind.

The Indians in and around Cape Flattery, on the Pacific coast of British North America, retain the urine dance in an unusually repulsive form. As was learned from Mr. Kennard, U.S. Coast Survey, whom the writer had the pleasure of meeting in Washington, D.C., in 1886, the medicine men distill, from potatoes and other ingredients, a vile liquor, which has an irritating and exciting effect upon the kidneys and bladder. Each one who has partaken of this dish immediately urinates and passes the result to his next neighbor, who drinks. The effect is as above, and likewise a temporary insanity or delirium, during which all sorts of mad capers are carried on. The last man who quaffs the poison, distilled through the persons of five or six comrades, is so completely overcome that he falls in a dead stupor.

8.

Cow Dung

and

Cow Urine

in

Religion

N *Coûtumes et Cérémonies Religieuses* (*Religious Customs and Ceremonies*), Bernard Picart narrates that the Brahmins fed grain to a sacred cow, and afterward searched in the ordure for the sacred grains, which they picked out whole, drying and administering them to the sick, not merely as a medicine, but as a sacred thing.

Not only among the people of the lowlands, but among those of the foot-hills of the Himalayas as well, do these rites find place. In Short's "Notes of the Hill Tribes of the Neilgherris," it says that "the very dung of the cow is eaten as an atonement for sin, and its urine is used in worship."

Michael Etmuller says that the Benjani, an Oriental sect, believers in the Transmigration of Souls, save the dung of their cows, gathering it up in their hands.

In *Siberia,* Georg Erman states that "Hindu merchants in Bokhara now lament loudly at the sight of a piece of cow's flesh, and at the same time mix with their food, that it may do them good, the urine of a sacred cow, kept in that place."

Edward Moor's *Hindu Pantheon* relates, "The greatest, or, at any rate, the most convenient of all purifiers is the urine of a cow. Images are sprinkled with it. No man of any pretensions to piety or cleanliness would pass a cow in the act of staling without receiving the holy stream in his hand and sipping a few drops. If the animal be retentive, a pious expectant will impatiently apply his finger, and by judicious tickling excite the grateful flow."

Captain Henri Jouan of the French Navy writes in a personal letter: "Forty years ago, during a stay of three months in Bombay, I saw frequently cows wandering in the streets, and Hindu devotees bowing, and lifting up the tails of the cows, rubbing the wombs of the aforesaid with the right hand, and afterwards rubbing their own faces with it."

Almost identical information was communicated by General J. J. Dana (U.S. Army) who, in the neighborhood of Calcutta, over forty years ago, had seen Hindu devotees besmeared from head to foot with human excrement.

In one of the Hindu fasts, the devotee adopts these disgusting excreta as his food, according to *Indian Antiquities* by Thomas Maurice. On the fourth day, "his disgusting beverage is the urine of the cow; the fifth, the excrement of that holy animal is his allotted food."

Speaking of the sacrifice called *Poojah,* Maurice says further: "The Brahman prepares a place, which is purified with dried cow-dung, with which the pavement is spread, and the room is sprin-kled with the urine of the same animal.''

Regarding the installation of Yudhisthira, who became Maha-rajah after the defeat and death of the Kauravas on the field of Kuruk-shetra, the Brahminical authors of the *Maha-Bharata* describe among the ceremonies used on that occasion the follow-ing one: ''After this, the five purifying articles which are produced from the sacred cow—namely, milk, the curds, ghee, the urine, and ordure—were brought up by Krishna and the Maharaja and by the brothers of Yudhisthira, and poured by them over the heads of Yudhisthira and Draupadi.''

Abbé Dubois, in his chapter ''Restoration to the Caste,'' says that a Hindu penitent ''must drink the *panchakaryam*—a word which literally signifies the five things, namely, milk, butter, curd, dung, and urine, all mixed together.'' And he adds: ''The urine of the cow is held to be the most efficacious of any for purifying all imaginable uncleanness. I have often seen the superstitious Hindu accompanying these animals when in the pasture, and watching the moment for receiving the urine as it fell, in vessels which he had brought for the purpose, to carry it home in a fresh state; or, catching it in the hollow of his hand, to bedew his face and all his body. When so used, it removes all external impurity, and when taken internally, which is very common, it cleanses all within.''

Very frequently, the excrement is first reduced to ashes. The monks of Chivem, called Pandarones, smear their faces, breasts, and arms with the ashes of cow dung; they run through the streets demanding alms, very much as the Zuñi actors demanded a feast, and chant the praises of Chivem, while they carry a bundle of peacock feathers in the hand, and wear the *lingam* at the neck.

In *Zoological Mythology*, De Gubernatis speaks of "the superstitious Hindu custom of purifying one's self by means of the excrement of a cow. The same custom passed into Persia; and the *Kharda Avesta* has preserved the formula to be recited by the devotee while he holds in his hand the urine of an ox or cow, preparatory to washing his face with it: 'Destroyed, destroyed, be the Demon Ahriman, whose actions and works are cursed.' "

The author continues, "We must complete the explanation of another myth, that of the excrement of the cow considered as purifying. The moon, as aurora, yields ambrosia. It is considered to be a cow; the urine of this cow is ambrosia or holy water. He who drinks this water purifies himself, as the ambrosia which rains from the lunar ray and the aurora purifies and makes clear the path of the sky, which the shadows of night darken and contaminate. The same virtue is attributed, moreover, to cow's dung, a conception also derived from the cow, and given to the moon as well as to the morning aurora. These two cows are considered as making the earth fruitful by means of their ambrosial excrements; these excrements being also luminous, both those of the moon and those of the aurora are considered as purifiers. The ashes of these cows, which their friend the heroine preserves, are not ashes, but golden powder or golden flour which, mixed with excrement, brings good fortune to the cunning robber-hero."

Professor W. Robertson Smith communicates in a personal letter: "It may be noted, according to Lajarde, 'cow's water' originally meant rain-water, the clouds being spoken of as cows. I give this for what it is worth."

This veneration for the excrement of the cow is to be found among other races. In *Heart of Africa,* Schweinfurth says, "Every idea and thought of the Dinka is how to acquire and maintain cattle. A certain kind of reverence would seem to be paid them; even their offal is considered of high importance. The dung, which is burnt to ashes for sleeping in and for smearing their persons, and the urine, which is used for washing and as a substitute for salt, are their daily requisites."

Among the superstitious practices of the Greeks, Plutarch mentions "rolling themselves in dung-hills." Plutarch also mentions "foul expiations," "vile methods of purgations," "bemirings at the temple," and speaks of "penitents wrapped up in foul and nasty rags," or "rolling naked in the mire," and "vile and abject adorations."

9.

ORDURE
ALLEGED TO HAVE BEEN USED

in

FOOD

by the

ISRAELITES

MONG THE BANIANS OF INDIA, PROSELYTES ARE obliged by the Brahmans to eat cow-dung for six months. They begin with one pound daily, and diminish from day to day. A subtle commentator, says Bernard Picart, might institute a comparison between the nourishment of these fanatics and the dung of cows which the Lord ordered the prophet Ezekiel to mingle with his food.

This was the opinion held by Voltaire on this subject. Speaking of the prophet Ezekiel, he said: "He is to eat bread of barley, wheat, beans, lentils, and millet, and to cover it with human excrement." It is thus, he says, that the "children of Israel shall eat their bread defiled among the nations among which they shall be banished." But "after having eaten this bread of affliction, God permits him to cover it with the excrement of cattle simply."

For mere filth, what can be fouler than 2 Kings XVIII, 27, Isaiah

XXXVI, 12, or Ezekiel IV, 12–15 (where the Lord changes human ordure into 'cow chips')?

In the *Philosophical Dictionary,* Henri Bayle does not allude to the baking of bread with ordure in his brief article upon the prophet Ezekiel; neither does Prof. J. Stuart Blaikie in his more comprehensive dissertation in the *Encyclopaedia Britannica.*

"The use of dung by the ancient Israelites is collected incidentally from the passage in which the prophet Ezekiel, being commanded, as a symbolic action, to bake his bread with dung, excuses himself from the use of an unclean thing, and is permitted to employ cow's dung instead." This is taken from Strong and McClintock's *Cyclopaedia of Biblical and Classical Literature.*

This view entertained by some biblical commentators is that the excrement was used for baking the bread; but if this be true, why should human faeces be used for such a purpose?

According to J. G. Forlong's *Rivers of Life,* "Ezekiel says that his God told him to lie for three hundred and ninety days on his left side, and then forty days on his right side, when 'he would lay hands on him and turn him from one side to another'; also that during all this period he was only to eat barley bread baked in too disgusting a manner to be described."

"This last command was, however, so strongly resented that his Deity somewhat relaxed it."

The most rational explanation of this much-disputed and ambiguous passage must necessarily be such as can be deduced from a consideration of Ezekiel's environment.

Giving due weight to every doubt, there remains this feature:

the prophet unquestionably was influenced and actuated by the ideas of his day and generation, which looked upon the humiliations to which he subjected himself as the outward manifestations of an inward spirituality.

Psychologically speaking, there is no great difference between the consumption of human excrement and the act of lying on one's side for three hundred and ninety days; both are indications of the same perverted cerebration, mistaken with such frequency for piety and holiness.

"Isaiah had periods of indecent maniacal outbursts; for we are told that he once went about stark naked for three years, because so commanded by the Lord." This is derived from *Rivers of Life* quoting Isaiah, XX. 2, 3.

Robertson Smith writes in a personal letter, "I fear that Voltaire cannot be taken as an authority on Hebrew matters. I believe that the passage from Ezekiel is correctly rendered in the revised edition, where at verse 15 'thereon' is substituted for 'therewith' of the old version. The use of dried cow's-dung as fuel is common among the poorer classes in the East; and in a siege, fuel, always scarce, would be so scarce that a man's dung might have to be used. I do not think that one need look further for the explanation of verses 15–17; the words of Verse 15 are not ambiguous, and that use for dung is the same as the Arabs still apply to the dried cakes of cow's dung used for fuel. Voltaire and Picart both seem to have used the Vulgate, in which Verse 12 is wrongly rendered."

10.

Excrement Gods

of

Romans

and

Egyptians

The Romans and Egyptians went farther than this. They had gods of excrement, whose special function was the care of latrines and those who frequented them. Torquemada, a Spanish author of high repute, expresses this in very plain language in *Monarchia Indiana*:

"I assert that they used *to adore* (as St. Clement writes to St. James the Less) stinking and filthy privies and water-closets; and, what is viler and yet more abominable, and an occasion for our tears and not to be borne with or so much as mentioned by name, they adored the noise and wind of the stomach when it expels from itself any cold or flatulence; and other things of the same kind, which, according to the same saint, it would be a shame to name or describe."

In the preceding lines, Torquemada refers to the Egyptians only, but, his language is almost the same when speaking of the Romans. The Roman goddess was called Cloacina. She was one of the first of the Roman deities, and is believed to have been named by Romulus himself. Under her charge were the various cloacae, sewers, privies, etc., of the Eternal City.

There is another opinion concerning Cloacina–that she was one of the names given to a statue of Venus found in the Cloaca Maxima. William Smith, in *Dictionary of Antiquities,* expresses this view, and it seems to be followed by the American and Britannic encyclopaedias. Lemprière defines Cloacina: "A goddess of Rome who presided over the Cloacae–some suppose her to be Venus– whose statue was found in the Cloacae, whence the name."

The Romans also had a god of ordure named Stercutius. Antione Banier's *Mythology* states: "Sterculius was one of the surnames given to Saturn because he was the first that had laid dung upon lands to make them fertile."

According to the *Bibliotheca Scatologica,* "The ancients had created many gods of excrement: 1. Stercus or Sterces, the father of Picus, inventor of the method of fertilizing the soil (St. Augustine, *De Civitate Dei*). 2. Sterculius (Macrobius, *Saturnalia*); 3. Stercutius (Lactantius, *De Falsa Religione*), Stercutus, Sterquilinus, Sterquiline, divinities who preside over fertilizing. Some persons believe that it was the surname of Saturn to designate him as the inventor of agriculture; others recognize him as the earth itself. Pliny states that this god was the son of the God Faunus and the grandson of Picus, the king of the Latins."

The Mexicans had a goddess, of whom we read the following. Father Fabreya says, in his commentary on the *Codex Borgianus,* that the mother of the human race is there represented in a state of humiliation, eating *cuitlatl* (*kopros,* Greek). The vessel in the left hand of Suchiquecal contains *mierda,* according to the interpreter of these paintings.

The Spanish *mierda,* like the Greek *kopros,* means *ordure.*

Besides Suchiquecal, the mother of the gods, who has been represented as eating excrement in token of humiliation, the Mexicans had other deities whose functions were more or less clearly complicated with alvine dejections. The most prominent of these was Ixcuina called also, Tlaçolteotl, the goddess of ordure, or Tlaçolquani, the *eater of ordure,* because she presided over loves and carnal pleasures.

In *Icazbalceta,* Geronimo de Mendieta mentions her as masculine, and in these terms: "The god of vices and dirtinesses, whom they called Tlazulteotl."

H. H. Bancroft speaks in *Native Races* of "the Mexican goddess of carnal love, called Tlaçolteotl, Ixcuina, Tlaçloquani," etc., and says that she "had in her service a crowd of dwarfs, buffoons, and hunchbacks, who diverted her with their songs and dances and acted as messengers to such gods as she took a fancy to." The last name of this goddess means "eater of filthy things," referring, it is said, to her function of hearing and pardoning the confessions of men and women guilty of unclean and carnal crimes.

In the manuscript explaining the *Codex Talleriano,* given in Lord Kingsborough's *Mexican Antiquities,* occurs the name of the goddess Ochpaniztli, whose feast fell on the 12th of September of our calendar. She was described as "the one who sinned by eating the fruit of the tree." The Spanish monks styled her, as well as another goddess, Tlaçolteotl–"*La diosa de basura ó pecado.*" But *basura* is not the alternative of sin (*pecado*); it means "dung, manure, ordure, excrement." According to the Dictionary of the Spanish Academy, the meaning is "the dirt and refuse collected in sweeping–the sweepings and dung of stables." It is possible that, in their zeal to discover analogies between the Aztec and Christian religions, the early missionaries passed over a number of points now left to conjecture.

In the same volume of Kingsborough, there is an allusion to the offerings or sacrifices made *Tepeololtec*, "*que, en romance, quiere decir sacrificios de mierda,*" which, "in plain language, signifies sacrifices of excrement." Nothing further can be adduced upon the subject, although a note at the foot of this page, in Kingsborough, says here several pages of the *Codex Talleriano* had been obliterated or mutilated, probably by some over-zealous expurgator.

Mr. John Frazer, LL.D., describing the ceremony of initiation, known to the Australians as the *Bora*, and which he defines to be "certain ceremonies of initiation through which a youth passes when he reaches the age of puberty to qualify him for a place among the men of the tribe and for the privileges of manhood. By these ceremonies he is made acquainted with his father's gods, the mythical lore of the tribe, and the duties required of him as a man. The whole is under the tutelage of a high spirit called 'Dharamoolun.' But, present at these ceremonies, although having no share in them, is an evil spirit called 'Gunungdhukhya,' i.e., 'eater of excrement,' whom the blacks greatly dread." Compare this word Gunungdhukhya, with the Sanskrit root-word *Gu*, i.e., excrement; *Dhuk* is the Australian "to eat."

Continuing his remarks upon the subject of the evil spirit Gunungdhukhya in his letter, he says: "This being is certainly supposed to eat ordure, and such is the meaning of his name."

Jacques Dulaure quotes from a number of authorities to show that the Israelites and Moabites had the same ridiculous and disgusting ceremonial in their worship of Bel-phegor. The devotee presented his naked posterior before the altar and relieved his entrails making an offering to the idol of the foul emanations.

Philo says the devotee of Baal-Peor presented to the idol all the outward orifices of the body. Another authority says that the worshipper not only presented all these to the idol, but that the emanations or excretions were also presented–tears from the eyes, wax from the ears, pus from the nose, saliva from the mouth, and urine and dejecta from the lower openings. This was the god to which the Jews joined themselves; and these, in all probability, were the ceremonies they practiced in his worship.

Still another authority says that the worshipper, presenting his bare posterior to the altar, relieved his bowels, and offered the result to the idol.

These citations go to show that the worshipper intended making not a merely ceremonial offering of flatulence, but an actual oblation of excrement, such as was placed upon the altars of their near neighbors, the Assyrians, in the devotions tendered to their Venus.

The Assyrian Venus had offerings of dung placed upon her altars. Another authority, Thomas Maurice, states in *Indian Antiquities* that "the zealous adorers of Siva rub the forehead, breast, and shoulders with ashes of cow-dung," and, further, he adds: "It is very remarkable that the Assyrian Venus, according to Lucian, had also offerings of dung placed upon her altars."

Knowing of the existence of "dung gods" among Romans, Egyptians, Hebrews, and Moabites, it is not unreasonable to insist, in the present case, upon a rigid adherence to the text, and to assert that, where it speaks of a sacrifice as a sacrifice of excrement and designates a deity as an eater of excrement, it means what it says, and should not be distorted, under the plea of symbolism, into a perversion of facts and ideas.

Some writers made out the name of the god Belzebul to be identical with Beelzebub, and to mean "Lord of Dung," but this interpretation is disputed by Schaff-Herzog's *Encyclopaedia of Religious Knowledge*.

In *Daemonologie*, King James gravely informs us that "Witches ofttimes confesse that in their worship of the Devil their form of adoration to be the kissing of his hinder parts." This book appeared with a commendatory preface from Hinton, one of the bishops of the English Church.

11.

LATRINES

HE MENTION OF THE ROMAN GODDESS CLOA-
cina suggests an inquiry into the general history of
latrines and urinals. Their introduction cannot be
ascribed to purely hygienic considerations, since
many nations of comparatively high development
have managed to get along without them; while,
on the other hand, tribes in low stages of culture have resorted to
them.

Heliogabalus was killed in one (latrine); Arius, the great here-
siarch, and Pope Leo, his antagonist, had the same fate. Charles
the Fifth, Emperor of Germany and Spain, was born in one in the
palace of Ghent, of Jeanne of Aragon, in 1500. Hence, they must
have been introduced in the localities named.

The Trojans defecated in the full light of day, if we can credit
the statement made to that effect in the *Bibliotheca Scatologica,* p. 8,
in which it is shown that a French author (name not given) wrote
a facetious but erudite treatise upon this subject.

In ancient Rome there were public latrines, but no privies attached to houses. There were basins and tubs, which were emptied daily by servants detailed for the purpose. No closet-paper was in use, as may be imagined, none having yet been invented or introduced in Europe, but in each public latrine, there was a bucket filled with salt water, and a stick having a sponge tied to one end, with which the passer-by cleansed his person, and then replaced the stick in the tub. Seneca, in his Epistle No. 70, describes the suicide of a German slave who rammed one of these sticks down his throat.

Obscene poetry was known in latrines in Rome as in our own day, and some of the compositions have come down to us.

Reverend John James Blunt informs his readers in *Vestiges of Ancient Manners and Customs* that the Romans protected their walls "against such as commit nuisances by consecrating the walls so exposed with the picture of a deity or some other hallowed emblem, and by denouncing the wrath of heaven against those who should be impious enough to pollute what it was their duty to reverence. The figure of a snake, it appears, was sometimes employed for this purpose. The snake, it is well known, was reckoned among the gods of the heathens."

John Mason Good says in a footnote to his translation to Lucretius: "Urinary reservoirs were erected in the streets of Rome, either for the purpose of public cleanliness, or for the use of the fullers, who were accustomed to purchase their contents from the Roman government during the reign of Vespasian, and perhaps other emperors, at a certain annual impost, and which, prior to the invention or general use of soap, was the substance employed principally in their mills for cleansing cloths and stuffs previous to their being dyed." In *Encyclopedia of Antiquities,* Fosbroke adds: "Vases, called *Gastra,* for the relief of passengers, were placed by the Romans upon the edges of roads and streets."

There must have been latrines in Scotland because James I of that kingdom was killed in one in the Monastery of the Black Friars, in Perth, in A.D. 1437; yet for many years later pedestrians in the streets of Edinburgh, after night-fall, took their own risks of the filthy deluge which house-maids were wont to pour down from the windows of the lofty houses.

According to Tobias Smollett in *Humphrey Clinker,* "And behold, there is nurra *goaks* in the whole kingdom (Scotland), nor anything for pore servants, but a barrel with a pair of tongs thrown across, and all the chairs of the family are emptied into this here barrel once a day; and at ten o'clock at night the whole cargo is flung out of a back windere that looks into some street or lane, and the maid calls, 'Gardy loo!' to the passengers, which signifies, 'Lord have mercy upon you!' and this is done every night in every house in Hadinborough."

The above seems to have been a French expression—"*Gare de l'eau*" ("Look out for the water!").

Privies were ordered for each house in Paris in 1513, whence we may infer that some house-builders had previously of their own impulse added such conveniences. As early as 1372, and again in 1395, there were royal ordinances forbidding the throwing of ordure out of the windows in Paris, which gives us the right to conclude that the custom must have been general and offensive. The same dispositions were taken for the city of Bordeaux.

Captain Cook tells us that the New Zealanders had privies to every three or four of their houses. He also takes occasion to say that there were no privies in Madrid until 1760; that the determination of the king to introduce them and sewers, and to prohibit the throwing of human ordure out of windows after nightfall, as had been the custom, nearly precipitated a revolution.

The addition of privies to the homes of the gentry would appear to have been an innovation in the time of Queen Elizabeth, else there would not have been so much comment made upon the action of Sir John Harington, her distant cousin, who erected one as a fitting convenience to his new house, near Bath, and published a very Rabelaisian volume upon the subject in London in 1596. The title of the book, being quite long—*A Discourse on a Stale Subject, called the Metamorphosis of Ajax.* From the description of the latrine in question, there is no doubt that Harington anticipated nearly all the mechanism of modern days.

According to Harington, Richard III is represented as having been seated in a latrine, "sitting on a draught," when he was "devising with Terril how to have his nephews privily murdered."

Henry Thomas Buckle's *Commonplace Book* offers the following incident: "In the *Chronicle of London,* written in the fifteenth century, a curious anecdote is related, to the effect that in A.D. 1258–60, a Jew, on Saturday, fell into a 'privy' at Tewksbury, but out of reverence for his Sabbath, would not allow himself to be drawn out. The next day being Sunday, the Earl of Gloucester would not let any one draw him out; and so, says the *Chronicle,* the Jew died in the privy."

John Frazer states in a personal letter: "The Rabbinical Jews believed that every privy was the abode of an unclean spirit of an excrement-eating god which could be inhaled with the breath, and descending into the lower parts of the body, lodge there, and thus like the Bhutas of India, bring suffering and disease."

Speaking of the Essenes, Josephus informs us in *Wars of the Jews*: "On the seventh day, they will not even remove any vessel out of its place, nor perform the most pressing necessities of nature. Nay, on other days they dig a small pit, a foot deep, with a paddle (which kind of hatchet is given them when they first are admitted among them), and, covering themselves round with their garment, that they may not affront the divine rays of light, they ease themselves into that pit. After which they put the earth that was dug out again into that pit. And even this they do only in the most lonesome places, which they choose for this purpose. And it is a rule with them to wash themselves afterwards, as if it were a defilement."

In Deuteronomy XXIII, it says: "And thou shalt have a paddle upon thy weapon; and it shall be, when thou wilt ease thyself abroad, thou shalt dig therewith, and shalt turn back and cover that which cometh from thee. For the Lord, thy God, walketh in the midst of thy camp, to deliver thee and to give up thine enemies before thee. Therefore shall thy camp be holy; that he see no unclean thing in thee, and turn away from thee."

Mr. John F. Mann confirms from personal observation that the natives of Australia observed the injunction given to the Hebrews. "From personal observation, I can state that the natives, all over the country, as a rule, are particular in this matter, but it was many years before I ascertained the reasons for this care. Sorcery and witchcraft exist in every tribe; each tribe has its *Kooradgee* or medicine-man. The natives imagine that any death, accident, or pain, is caused by the evil influence of some enemy. These *Kooradgees* have the power not only of inflicting pain, but of causing all kinds of trouble. They are particular to always carry about with them, in a net bag, a 'charm' which is most ordinarily made of rock crystal, human excrement, and kidney fat. If one of these medicine-men can obtain possession of some of the excrement of his intended victim, or some of his hair, in fact anything belonging to his person, it is the most easy thing in the world to bewitch him. The disposal of excreta is not so much for the sake of cleanliness as to prevent any human substance from falling into the hands of the enemy."

The same custom has been ascribed to the Dyaks of Borneo. It is by no means certain that this custom had its origin in any suggestion of cleanliness; on the contrary, it is fully probable that the idea was to avert the maleficence of witchcraft by putting out of sight material the possession of which would give witches so much power over the former owner.

Padre Gumilla says that the Indians on the Orinoco have the same custom as the Jews and the Turks have of digging holes with a hoe and covering up their evacuations. No such cleanliness can be attributed to the Indians of the Plains of North America or the nomadic tribes of the Southwest.

Arminius Vambéry reports in *Sketches of Central Asia*: "By the Mahometan law, the body becomes unclean after each evacuation. Both greater and smaller requires an ablution, according to circumstances. If a drop of urine touches the clothes, they must be washed." For fear that their garments have been so defiled, "the

Bokhariots frequently repeat their prayers stark naked." The manner of cleaning the body after an evacuation of any kind is defined by religious ritual. "The law commands *istindjah* (removal), *istinkah* (ablution), and *isitibra* (drying)"—i.e., a small clod of earth is first used for the local cleansing, then water at least twice, and finally a piece of linen a yard in length. In Turkey, Arabia, and Persia, all are necessary, and pious men carry several clods of earth for the purpose in their turbans.

Moslems urinate sitting down on their heels "for a spray of urine would make hair and clothes ceremonially impure. After urinating, the Moslem wipes the os penis with one to three bits of stone, clay, or a handful of earth, and he must perform *Wuzu* before he can pray." In *A Voyage to the Levant,* Tournefort tells a pleasant story about certain Christians at Constantinople who powdered with *poivre d'Inde* (Indian pepper) the stones in a wall where the Moslems were in the habit of rubbing the os penis by way of wiping.

Speaking of the Mahometans, Tournefort says, "When they make water, they squat down like women, for fear some drops of urine should fall into their breeches. To prevent this evil, they squeeze the part very carefully, and rub the head of it against the wall; and one may see the stones worn in several places by this custom. To make themselves sport, the Christians smear the stones sometimes with Indian pepper and the root called 'Calf's-Foot' (ginger), or some other hot plants, which frequently causes an inflammation in such as happen to use the Stone. As the pain is very smart, the poor Turks commonly run for a cure to those very Christian surgeons who were the authors of all the mischief. They never fail to tell them it is a very dangerous case, and that they should be obliged, perhaps, to make an amputation. The Turks, on the contrary, protest and swear that they have had no communication with any sort of woman that could be suspected. In short, they wrap up the suffering part in a Linen dipped in Oxicrat (wine vinegar and water) tinctured with a little Bole-Armenic; and this they sell them as a great specifik for this kind of Mischief.''

Schurig's *Chylologia* devotes a long paragraph to an exposition of the views entertained by learned physicians in regard to the effects to be expected from the deposition of the fecal matter upon plants that were either noxious or beneficial to the human organism. In the former case, the worst results were to be dreaded from sympathy; in the latter only the most salutary. Rustics, in his opinion, enjoyed better health than the inhabitants of cities for the very peculiar reason that the latter evacuated in latrines and in the act were compelled to inhale the deleterious gases emanating from the foul deposits already accumulated; whereas the countryman could go out to a comfortable place in the fields and evacuate without the danger and inconvenience to which the urban population were subject. But he takes occasion to warn his readers that they must be careful not to defecate upon certain malignant herbs which might be the cause of virulent dysentery.

There are no latrines of any kind in Angola; the Negroes believe that it is very vile to frequent the same place for such purposes. They do not cover up their excrements, but deposit them out in the bushes. Sometimes it happens that a man will defecate inside the house, in which case he will be laughed at all the rest of his life, and be called *D'Kombe,* which is a kind of leopard.

Dr. Henry Barth gives a description of Timbuctoo in *Travels in North and Central Africa*: "I was disgusted with the custom which prevailed in the houses like that in which I was lodged of using the terrace as a sort of closet; and I had great difficulty in preventing my guide, Amer el Walati, who still stayed with me and made the terrace his usual residence, from indulging in the filthy practice."

Master Richard Jobson's *Gold Coast of Africa* tells of the inhabitants as follows: "When they ease themselves, they commonly go in the morning unto the Towne's end, where there is a place purposely made for them, that they may not bee seene, so also because men passing by should not be molested with the smell thereof. They also esteeme it a bad thing that men should ease themselves upon the ground, and therefore they make houses which are borne up above the ground, wherein they ease themselves upon the ground, and every time they do it they wipe; or else they goe to the water's side and ease themselves in the sand; and when the Privie houses are full, they set fire to them, and let them burn to ashes."

In *Voyage Round the World,* Forster says of the inhabitants of the Marquesas Islands: "They are peculiarly cleanly in regard to the egestae. At the Society Islands, the wanderer's eyes and nose are offended every morning in the midst of a path with the natural effects of a sound digestion; but the natives of the Marquesas are accustomed, after the manner of our cats, to bury the offensive objects in the earth. At Tahiti, indeed, they depend on the friendly assistance of rats, who greedily devour these odoriferous dainties; nay, they seem to be convinced that their custom is the most proper in the world; for their witty countryman, Tupaya, found fault with our want of delicacy when he saw a small building appropriated to the rites of Cloacina in every house in Batavia."

Alfred Russel Wallace reports about the habits of the natives in *The Malay Archipelago:* "The aspect of the village itself is very neat, the ground being often swept before the chief houses; but very bad odors abound, owing to there being under each house a stinking mud-hole, formed by all waste liquids and refuse matter poured down through the floor above. In most other things, Malays are tolerably clean—in some scrupulously so—and this peculiar and nasty custom, which is almost universal, arises, I have little doubt, from their having been originally a water-loving and maritime people, who built their houses on posts in the water, and only migrated gradually inland, first up the rivers and streams, and then into the dry interior. Habits which were once so convenient and cleanly, and which had been so long practised as to become a part of the domestic life of the nation, were of course continued when the first settlers built their houses inland; and, without a regular system of drainage, the arrangement of the villages is such that any other system would be very inconvenient."

Dr. Joseph Porter communicates the information that he has often heard the Arctic explorer Dr. Hayes speak of the propensity of the Eskimo off the east coast of Greenland to use the trench to the hut as a latrine. He tried in vain to prevent this practice among his Eskimo attendants, but believed that they had a pride among themselves in leaving conspicuous traces of their presence.

In *Voyage to Iceland and Greenland,* Dittmar Bleeckens gives this account: "Neither is it lawfull for any one to rise from the table to make water; but for this purpose the daughter of the house, or another maid or woman, attendeth always at the table, watchfull if any one beckon to them. To him that beckoneth shee gives the chamber-pott under the table with her owne hands; the rest in the meanwhile grunt like swine least any noise bee heard. The water being poured out, hee washeth the bason, and offereth his services to him that is willing; and he is accounteth uncivill who abhorreth this fashion."

According to Franz Boas, in the Eskimo myths there is the story of the Eskimo boy, an orphan, who was abused by being made to carry out of the hut the large urine vessel. This would indicate a certain antiquity for the employment of these vessels.

Van Stralenberg says of the Koraks in his *Historico-Geographical Description*: "For their necessary occasions they make use of a tub, which they have with them in the hut, and when full they carry it out, and make use of the same tub to bring in water for other occasions."

According to *Notes* of Richard Johnson, "The Tartars hold it not good to abide long in one place, for they will say when they will curse any of their children, 'I would thou mightest tarry so long in one place that thou mightest smell thine own dung as the Christians do'; and this is the greatest curse they have."

In *The Snake Dance of the Moquis of Arizona,* the author had something to say touching the practice of the Moquis, Zuñis, and others of the Pueblo tribes of collecting urine in vessels of earthenware. This was for the purpose of saving the fluid for use in dyeing the wool of which their blankets and other garments were to be made. It was noticed, however, that a particular place was assigned for such emergencies as might arise when the ordinary receptacles might not be within reach. Thus, in the town of Hualpi on the eastern mesa in the northeast of the Territory of Arizona, one of the corners had been in such constant use and for so long a time that the stream percolating down from the wall had eroded a channel for itself in the friable sandstone flooring, which would serve to demonstrate that the place had been so dedicated for a very extended number of years.

It is also related that immigrants to California from the States of Missouri and Arkansas, for some reason not understood, had the singular custom of burning their own excrement in the camp-fire.

One reads in *The Travels of Two Mahometans through India and China* that, among the Chinese, "it is usual for the princes, and even the people, to make water standing. Persons of dignity, as well as the vice-kings, and the principal officers, have gilded canes, a cubit long, which are bored through, and these they use as often as they make water, standing upright all the time; and by this means the tube carries the water to a good distance from them. They are of the opinion that all pains in the kidneys, the strangury, and even the stone, are caused by making water in a sitting posture; and that the reins cannot free themselves absolutely of these humors but by standing to evacuate; and that thus this posture contributes exceedingly to the preservation of health."

Carl Lumholtz stated that the Australian men squatted while urinating; the women generally stood erect, but upon this point he was not quite sure. Lumholtz also stated to the author that the Australians urinate in the presence of strangers, and while talking to them.

According to Herodotus, the Egyptian "women stand up when they make water, but the men sit down."

The author has seen an Italian woman of the lower class urinating in this manner in the street near San Pietro in Vinculis, Rome in open daylight in 1883.

Harington states that "among the Turks, it is a heresy to piss standing."

Old women in Switzerland urinate standing, especially in cold weather.

12.

AN INQUIRY

into the

NATURE OF THE RITES
CONNECTED WITH THE WORSHIP

of

BEL-PHEGOR

T MAY BE WELL TO BEAR IN MIND THAT THE heathen idea of the power of a god was entirely different from our own. The deities of the heathen were restricted in their powers and functions; they were assigned to the care of certain countries, districts, valleys, rivers, fountains, etc. Not only that, they were capable of aiding only certain trades, professions, etc. They were not able to cure all diseases, only particular kinds, each god being a specialist; consequently, each was supposed to take charge of a section of the human body. This was the case with the Greeks, Romans, Egyptians, and others. In medieval times, the same rule obtained, only in place of gods, we find saints assigned to these functions. Brand's *Popular Antiquities* gives a list of the saints, and the functions ascribed to each. Here, it will be seen that Saint Erasmus was in charge of "the belly, with the entrayles." Keeping this in view, we can better understand the peculiar ceremonies connected with the worship of Bel-Phegor. He was, no

doubt, the deity to whom the devotee resorted for the alleviation of ailments connected with the rectum and belly, much as he would, at a later date in the history of religion, have invoked Saint Phiacre to relieve him "of the phy or emeroids, of those especially which grow in the fundament." On the same principle that the worshipper was wont to hang up in the temples of Esculapius wax and earthen representations of the sore arms, legs, and other members which gave him pain, the worshipper of Bel-Phegor would offer him the sacrifice of the flatulence and excrement, testimonies of the good health for which gratitude was due to the older deity.

According to Purchas' *Pilgrims,* "Origen saith the name Baal-Peor signifieth filthiness, but what filthiness he knew not. Salomon Ben Jarchi writeth they offered to him ordure, placing before his mouth the likeness of that place which Nature hath made for egestion."

The *Bibliotheca Scatologica* is a curious collection of learning, no name and no place of publication of which can be found, but which seems to have been printed by Giraudet et Jouaust, 315 Rue Saint Honoré, Paris, granting that this title be not fictitious. In that work are to be seen the titles of no less than one hundred and thirty-three treatises upon Flatulence, some grotesque, some coarse, one or two of quaint erudition. For instance, the celebrated English orator, Charles James Fox, is credited with the authorship of "An Essay upon Wind," published anonymously in London, and numbered 91 in the *Bibliotheca Scatologica.*

This collection also relates: "The Fart was a divinity of the ancient Egyptians. It was the personification of a natural function. They figured it as a very young child bending over who seems to be making a great effort, and one can see this representation in many works of antiquity. The poem by Calotin with the title 'Le Conseil de Momus' 'The Plan of Momus' gives two versions of this god. The author of the *Dissertation sur un Ancien Usage* contests that these figures have anything to do with the god Crepitus, and believes rather that they must have been invented for a more respectable purpose."

Charles Perry recalls in *A View of the Levant*: "The ancient Pelusiens, a people of lower Egypt, did venerate a Fart, which they worshipped under the symbol of a swelled paunch."

The interview between Moses and Jehovah, where the latter refused to allow the prophet to see the glory of his face, but made him content himself with a view of his posterior, indicates that the sacred writers of the earlier periods were living in an atmosphere of thought which accepted all such ideas as those surrounding the Bel-Phegorian ceremonials.

The Hebrews believed that Jehovah should be propitiated with sweet savors: "Offer up a sweet savor unto the Lord." Bel-Phegor and other deities of the gentiles, who were the gods of particular parts of the human body, would, in all probability, be pleased with oblations coming especially from that particular part. Thus, the god of Hunting had offerings of game; the gods of the Seas had sacrifices of fish; babies were offered to the deities of Childbirth. Therefore the gods of the fundament should, naturally, be regaled with excrement and flatulence.

The Parsis have a curious idea suggestive of the Hebrew antagonism to the worship of Bel-Phegor as described in the *Shapast la Shayast*: "The rule is that when one retains a prayer inwardly and wind shall come from below, or wind shall come from the mouth, it is all one." A footnote explains: "Literally, 'both are one,' that is, in either case the spell of the prayer is broken."

Richard Burton reports in *Arabian Nights*: "The Bedawi, who eructates as a matter of civility, has a mortal hatred to a *crepitus ventris*; and were a by-stander to laugh at its accidental occurrence, he would be at once cut down as a *pundonor*. The same is the custom among the Highlanders of Afganistan. And its artificial nature suggests direct derivation; for the two regions are separated by a host of tribes, Persians and Beloch, who utterly ignore the *pundonor* and behave like Europeans. The raids of the pre-Ishmaelitish Arabs over the lands lying to the northeast of them are almost forgotten. Still, there are traces, and this may be one of them."

According to Niebuhr, the voiding of wind is considered to be the gravest indecency among the Arabs. Some tribes make a perpetual butt of the offender once guilty of such an infraction of decorum. The Belludjages upon the frontiers of Persia expel the culprit from the tribe. Yet Niebuhr himself relates in *Description de l'Arabie* that a sheik of the tribe Montesids once had a contest of this kind among his henchmen and that he "crowned the victor."

Snoring and Flatulence would seem to have been equally offensive by the Tartars. See Marco Polo's reference in Purchas to the mode of selecting wives for the Grand Khan. He says that the Grand Khan puts those deemed to be eligible under the care of "his Baron's wives to see if they snore not in their sleepe, if in smell or behaviour they bee not offensive."

Master Richard Jobson says in the same book that the Negroes on the Gold Coast of Africa "are very careful not to let a fart, if anybody be by them. They wonder at our Netherlanders that use it so commonly, for they cannot abide that a man should fart before them, esteeming it to be a great shame and contempt done unto them."

Bastian quotes from Kubary's *Religion of the Pelew Islands* to the effect that in cases of death, the vagina, urethra, rectum, nostrils, and all other orifices of the body are tightly closed with the fibers of certain roots or sponge, to prevent the escape of any of the liquids of the body, which seem to be of some use to the spirit of the deceased.

Suetonius has the following remarks upon the Roman Emperor Claudius: "It is said too that he intended to publish an edict allowing to all people the liberty of giving vent at table to any distension occasioned by flatulence." This was upon "hearing of a person whose modesty, under such circumstances, had nearly cost him his life."

The *Bibliotheca Scatologica* says, "Cicero considered the Fart as an innocent victim that was oppressed by the civilization of his time. Therefore he let out a cry of freedom to his pleasure and exercised his right." As a footnote to the foregoing we read the following extract from Cicero: "*Crepitus aeque liberos ac ructus esse opportere.*" "The fart as much as the burp must be permitted in the same way."

Plutarch asks the question: "Why was it ordained that they who were to live chaste should obstain from pulse? Or rather was it because they should bring empty and slender bodies to their purifications and expiations? For pulse are windy and cause a great deal of excrements that require purging off. Or is it because they excite lechery by reason of their flatulent and windy nature?"

"Thunder is nothing more than a fart." Thus said Aristophanes in *The Clouds*.

Martial remarked, "I would prefer that you fart, because, as Symmachus says, that would be very useful, and, at the same time, this thing also stimulates laughter."

13.
Obscene Survivals *in the* Games *of the* English Rustics

THE ROUGH GAMES OF THE ENGLISH RUSTICS ARE not altogether free from vestiges of the same nature as have been recorded of the Arabian sheik in the preceding pages. For example, in Northumberland, England, there was a curious diversion called "F——ing for the Pig." Brand's *Popular Antiquites* gives no explanation of the custom, which may be allied to the worship of Bel-Phegor. Brand says: "The ancient coarseness of our manners would almost exceed belief. In the stage directions to the old Moralities we often find, 'Here Satan letteth a f——.' "

In London itself such "survivals" lingered down to very recent periods. Brand reports: "In former times the porters that plyed at Billingsgate used civilly to entreat and desire every man that passed that way to salute a post that stood there in a vacant place. If he refused to do this, they forthwith laid hold of him, and by main force bouped his——against the post; but if he quietly submitted to kiss the same, and paid down sixpence, then they gave him a name, and chose some one of the gang for his godfather. I believe this was done in memory of some old image that formerly stood there, perhaps of Belius or Belin."

All these customs, absurd as they seem to us, may have been parts of the ritual of deities of the same class as Bel-Phegor, who looked after the excreta perhaps, and the organs connected therewith. Some kind of a tribute was demanded, and none could be more appropriate than the offering of the parts or the submission to some pain inflicted upon them by those in charge of the shrine.

Crossing the Atlantic, a custom suspiciously like the preceding was still to be heard of as a rough boyish prank in Philadelphia thirty or more years ago. Whenever it happened that any boy was guilty of flatulence, all the party of school-boys would cry, "Touch wood!" and run to touch the nearest tree-box. Those who were slow in doing this were pounded by the more rapid ones.

The following memoranda from T. H. Buckle's *Commonplace Book* seem to have no value beyond merely filthy stories:

> *Ludlow's f— was a prophetique trump;*
> *There never was anything so jump;*
> *'T was a very type of a vote of this rump,*
> *Which nobody can deny.*

Ludlow is a staunch Republican. The incident alluded to was a subject of much merriment, and exercised the pens of some of the choicest poets of the latter half of the seventeenth century.

> *And then my poets,*
> *The same that writ so subtly of the fart.*
>   Ben Jonson, *The Alchemist*

Whalley comments: "Who the author alluded to should be I cannot say. In the collection of poems called *Facetiae: Musarum Deliciae, or The Muses' Recreation* by Sir John Mennis and Dr. James Smith, there is a poem called 'The Fart Censured in the Parliament House.' It was occasioned by an escape of that kind of the House of Commons. I have seen part of this poem ascribed to an author in the time of Elizabeth, and possibly it may be the thing referred to by Jonson." But Gifford, from whose later editions of Jonson I have drawn my material, comments to the effect that "this escape, as Whalley calls it, took place in 1607, long after the time of Elizabeth. The ballad is among the Harleian Manuscripts, and is also printed in the State Poems; it contains about forty stanzas of the most wretched doggerel."

Jack of Dover's *Quest of Inquiry* recites the tale of the Fool of Cornwall. "I was told of a humorous knight dwelling in the same countrey that is, Cornwall, who upon a time, having gathered together in one open market-place a great assemblie of knights, squires, gentlemen, and yeomen, and whilest they stood expecting to heare some discourse or speech to proceed from him, he, in a foolish manner not without laughter, began to use a thousand jestures, turning his eyes this way and then that way, seeming always as though presently he would have begun to speake, and at last, fetching a deepe sigh, with a grunt like a hogge, he let a beastly loud fart, and tould them that the occasion of this calling them together was to no other end but that so noble a fart might be honoured with so noble a company as there was."

He also mentions the Fool of Lincoln. "There dwelleth of late a certaine poore labouring man in Lincoln, who, upon a time, after his wife had so reviled him with tongue nettle as the whole streete rung again for weariness thereof, at last he went out of the house, and sate him downe quietly upon a blocke before his owne doore. His wife, being more out of patience by his quietness and gentle sufferaunce, went up into the chamber, and out at the window powred downe a pisse-pot upon his head; which when the poor man sawe, in a merry moode he spake these words: 'Now, surely,' quoth he, 'I thought at last that after so great a thunder we should have some raine.' "

The preceding filthy pleasantry comes down from a very distinguished origin. Harington's *Ajax* recalls the adventure of the "good Socrates, who, when Xantippe had crowned him with a chamberpot, he bore it off single with his head and shoulder, and said to such as laughed at it:

It never yet was deemed a wonder
To see that rain should follow thunder."

14.

URINE

and

ORDURE

in

INDUSTRIES

HE ECONOMICAL VALUE OF HUMAN AND ANIMAL excreta would seem to have obtained recognition among all races from the earliest ages. It is not venturing beyond limits to assert that a book could be written upon this phase of the subject alone. It is not essential to incorporate here all that could be compiled, but enough is submitted to substantiate the statement just made, and to cover every line of inquiry.

Havelock Ellis writes in a personal letter: "It certainly is not possible to separate the religious uses of urine from its industrial and medical uses. Probably nearly everywhere it has been the first soap known. Does not this aspect of the matter need to be insisted on, even from the religious point of view? In England and France, and probably elsewhere, the custom of washing the hands in urine, with the idea of its softening and beautifying influence, still subsists among ladies, and I have known those who constantly made water on their hands with this idea."

★ ★ ★

Tanning. The inhabitants of Kodiak employ urine in preparing the skins of birds, according to Uri Lisiansky.

By the Eskimo, urine is preserved for use in tanning skins, while its employment in the preparation of leather, in both Europe and America, is too well understood to require any reference to authorities.

The Kioways of the Great Plains soaked their buffalo hides in urine to make them soft and flexible.

Martin Sauer says that the Yakuts tan deer and elk skins with cow-dung.

Dung is used in tanning by the Bongo of the upper Nile region.

Bernal Diaz, in his enumeration of the articles for sale in the *tianguez* or market-places of Tenochtitlan, uses this expression in *Conquest of Mexico*: "I must also mention human excrements, which were exposed for sale in canoes lying in the canals near the square, which is used for the tanning of leather; for, according to the assurances of the Mexicans, it is impossible to tan well without it."

The same use of ordure in tanning bear-skins can be found among the nomadic Apaches of Arizona, although, preferentially, they use the ordure of the animal itself.

Dyeing. Urine is used in dyeing by the people of Ounalashka, according to Langsdorff's *Voyages*.

The same use of it has been attributed to the Irish by Camden in *Brittania* (London, 1753). His statement is quoted by Buckle in the *Commonplace Book*: "In 1562, O'Neal, with some of his com-

panions, came to London and astonished the citizens by their hair
flowing in locks on their shoulders, on which were yellow sur-
plices, dyed with saffron or stained with urine."

In *The Manners and Customs of the Ancient Irish*, Eugene O'Curry
explains further: "The preparation of blue, violet, and bluish-red
coloring matters from lichens by the action of the ammonia of stale
urine seems to have been known at a very early period to the
Mediterranean peoples, and the existence, down almost to the
present day, of such a knowledge in the more remote parts of
Ireland, Scotland, and Scandinavia, renders it not improbable that
the art of making such dyes was not unknown to the northern
nations of Europe also."

Plaster. As a plaster for the interior of dwellings, cow-dung has
been used with frequency; that the employment of the ordure of
an animal held sacred by so many peoples has a religious basis, is
perhaps too much to say, but it will be shown further on that
different ordures were kept about houses to ensure good luck or
to avert the maleficence of witchcraft.

Marco Polo has the following: "In Malabar, there are some
called Gaui, who eat such oxen as die of themselves, but may not
kill them, and daub over their houses with cow-dung."

According to Michel Adanson's *Voyage to Senegal,* the huts in
Senegal were plastered "with cow-dung which stunk abomina-
bly."

"The cow-dung basements around the tents" of the Mongols
are spoken of by Reverend James Gilmour in *Among the Mongols.*

Animal dung is used as a mortar by the inhabitants of Turkey in Asia living in the valley of the Tigris.

In *The Albert Nyanza,* Sir Samuel Baker says that the natives of the White Nile, the tribes of the Bari, make "a cement of ashes, cow-dung, and sand," with which "they plaster the floors and enclosures about their houses."

Pliny tells us that the threshing-floors of the Roman farmers were paved with cow-dung; in a footnote, it is stated that the same rule obtains in France to this day.

Mungo Park relates in *Travels in Africa:* "The people of Jungeion collected the dung of cows and sheep, dried it, roasted it on the fire, and afterwards used it for a bed."

As a Cure for Tobacco. The best varieties of Tobacco coming from America were arranged in bunches, tied to stakes, and suspended in privies, in order that the fumes arising from the human ordure and urine might correct the corrupt and noxious principles in the plant in the crude state.

Dr. Gustav Jaeger writes in a personal letter: "I heard lately from good authority that, in Havana, the female urine is used in cigar-manufacturing as a good maceration."

Cheese Manufacture. Jaeger also says, "A storekeeper in Berlin was punished some years ago for having used the urine of young girls with a view to make his cheese richer and more piquant. Notwithstanding, people went, bought and ate his cheese with delight. What may be the cause of all these foolish and mysterious things? In human urine is the Anthropin."

Whether or not the use of human urine to ripen cheese origi-nated in the ancient practice of employing excrementitious matter to preserve the products of the dairy from the maleficence of witches; or, on the other hand, whether or not such an employ-ment as an agent to defeat the efforts of the witches be traceable to the fact that stale urine was originally the active ferment to hasten the coagulation of the milk would scarcely be worth dis-cussion.

Opium Adulteration. The smoker of opium little imagines that, in using his deadly drug, he is often smoking an adulterated article, the adulterant being hen manure. He is thus placed on a par with the American Indian smoking the dried dung of the buffalo, and the African smoking that of the antelope or the rhinoceros.

Egg-Hatching. In the description of the province of Quang-tong by Du Halde in *History of China,* it is stated that the Chinese hatch eggs "in the Oven, or in Dung."

Chrysocollon. There was a cement for fixing the precious metals, which cement was known as *Chrysocollon,* and was made with much ceremony from the urine "of an innocent boy." There are various descriptions, but the following, while brief, contains all the material points.

Galen describes this Chrysocollon, or Gold-Glue, as prepared by some physicians from the urine of a boy, who had to void it into a mortar of red copper while a pestle of the same material was in motion, which urine carefully exposed to the sun until it had acquired the thickness of honey, was considered capable of soldering gold and of curing obstinate diseases.

For Removing Ink Stains. Human urine was considered efficacious in the removal of ink-spots.

As an Article of Jewelry. Fossilized excrement is used in the manufacture of jewelry, under the name of *Coprolite.*

Lapland women carry a little case made from the bark of the birch tree which, according to Knud Leems' *Account of Danish Lapland,* "they usually carry under the girdle" in which is to be found reindeer dung, not as an amulet but to aid in weaning the young reindeer by smearing the udders of the dams."

But, from other sources, we have learned that the Laps attached the most potent influences to ordure and urine, believing that their reindeer could be bewitched, that vessels could be hastened or retarded in their course, etc., by the use of such materials.

Tattooing. Georg Langsdorff noticed that urine entered into the domestic economy of the natives of Ounalashka. He tells us in *Voyages* that the tattooing was performed with "a sort of coal dust mixed with urine, rubbed in" the punctures made in the skin. That the tattooing with which savages decorate their bodies has a significance beyond a simple personal ornamentation cannot be gainsaid, although the degree of its degeneration from a primitive religious symbolism may now be impossible to determine.

★   ★   ★

Agriculture. In the interior of China, travellers relate that copper receptacles along the roadsides rescue from loss a fertilizer whose value is fully recognized.

The *Chinese Repository* states: "The dung of all animals is esteemed above any other kind of manure. It often becomes an article of commerce in the shape of small cakes, which are made by mixing it with a portion of loam and earth, and then thoroughly drying them. These cakes are even brought from Siam, and they also form an article of commerce between the provinces. They are never applied dry, but are diluted with as much animal water as can be procured."

Rosinus Lentilius in *Ephemeridum Physico-Medicorum* states that the people of China and Java buy human ordure in exchange for tobacco and nuts. This was probably on account of its value in manuring their fields, which, he tells us, was done three times a year with human ordure.

According to Kemper's *History of Japan,* "The Japanese manure their fields with human ordure."

G. W. Benjamin says in *Persia* that the finest variety of melon, the sugar melon, is "cultivated with the greatest care with the dung of pigeons kept for the purpose."

In *Cyclopaedia of Antiquities,* Fosbroke cites Tavernier as saying that the King of Persia draws a greater revenue from "the dung than from the pigeons" belonging to him in Ispahan. The Persians are said to live on melons during the summer months, and "to use pigeons' dung in raising them."

Human manure was best for fields, according to Pliny. Homer

relates that King Laertes laid dung upon his fields. Augeas was the first king among the Greeks so to use it, and "Hercules divulged the practice thereof among the Italians."

Urine was considered one of the best manures for vines. Pliny says: "Wounds and incisions of trees are treated also with pigeon's dung and swine manure. If pomegranates are acid, the roots of the trees are cleared, and swine's dung is applied to them. The result is that in the first year the fruit will have a vinous flavor, but in the succeeding one it will be sweet. The pomegranates should be watered four times a year with a mixture of human urine and water. For the purpose of preventing animals from doing mischief by browsing upon the leaves, they should be sprinkled with cow-dung each time after rain."

In *Comentarios Reales,* Garcillasso de la Vega states: "In the valley of Cuzco, Peru, and, indeed, in almost all parts of the Sierra, they used human manure for the maize crops, because they said it was the best."

Urine Used in the Manufacture of Salt. Gomara explains that, mixed with palm-scrapings, human urine served as salt for the Indians of Bogota.

Salt is made by the Latookas of the White Nile from the ashes of goat's dung.

The Siberians gave human urine to their reindeer. John Dundas Cochrane reports in *Pedestrian Journey Through Siberian Tartary:* "Nothing is so acceptable to a reindeer as human urine, and I have even seen them run to get it as occasion offered."

George Melville also relates that he saw the drivers urinate into the mouths of their reindeer in the Lena Delta.

Here the intent was evident. The animals needed salt, and no other method of obtaining it was feasible during the winter months. Cochrane is speaking of the Tchuktchi; but he was also among Yakuts and other tribes. He walked from St. Petersburg to Kamtschatka and from point to point in Siberia for a total distance of over six thousand miles.

Preparation of Sal Ammoniac and Phosphorus. Diderot and D'Alembert say in the *Encyclopaedia* that the sal ammoniac of the ancients was prepared with the urine of camels; that phosphorus, as then manufactured in England, was made with human urine, as was also saltpetre.

Edward Pocock comments in *Travels in Egypt*: "A notion has prevailed that sal ammoniac was made of the sand on which camels had staled, and that a great number going to the temple of Jupiter Ammon gave occasion for the name of ammoniac, corrupted to armoniac. Whether it ever could be made by taking up the sand and preparing it with fire, as they do with the dung at present, those who are best acquainted with the nature of these things will be best able to judge. I was informed that it was made of the soot which is caused by burning the dung of cows and other animals. The hotter it is the better it produces; and for that reason the dung of pigeons is the best. That of camels is also much esteemed."

Martin Schurig devotes a chapter of *Chylologia* to the medicinal preparations made from human ordure. In every case the ordure had to be that of a youth from twenty-five to thirty years old. This manner of preparing chemicals from the human excreta, including phosphorus from urine, was carried to such a pitch that some philosophers believed the philosopher's stone was to be found by mixing the salts obtained from human urine with those obtained from human excrement.

Manure Employed as Fuel. The employment of manures as fuel for firing pottery among Moquis, Zuñis, and other Pueblos, and for general heating in Thibet has been pointed out by the author in a former work, *The Snake Dance of the Moquis.* It was used for the same purpose in Africa, according to Mungo Park. The dung of the buffalo served the same purpose in the domestic economy of the Plains Indians. Camel dung is the fuel of the Bedouins; that of men and animals alike was saved and dried by the Syrians, Arabians, Egyptians, and people of West of England for fuel. Egyptians heated their lime-kilns with it.

Pocock's *Travels in Egypt* says this of camel dung: "In order to make fuel of it, they mix it, if I mistake not, with chopped straw, and, I think, sometimes with earth, and make it into cakes and dry it; and it is burnt by the common people in Egypt; for the wood they burn at Cairo is very dear, as it is brought from Asia Minor."

In *Travels to Discover the Source of the Nile,* James Bruce says that the Nuba of the villages called Daher, at the head of the White Nile, Abyssinia, "never eat their meat raw as in Abyssinia; but with the stalk of the dura or millet and the dung of camels they make ovens under ground, in which they roast their hogs whole, in a very cleanly and not disagreeable manner."

The dung of camels is the fuel of the Kirghis.

Yak manure is used as a fuel in Eastern Thibet, according to W. W. Rockhill.

Cow manure is employed for the same purpose by the people of Turkey in Asia, in the valley of the Tigris, near Mosul, according to George Smith.

The use of cow-dung as fuel in certain parts of the world would seem not to be entirely divested of the religious idea.

According to Francis Buchanan's *Journey through Mysore*: "Firewood at Seringapatam is a dear article, and the fuel most commonly used is cow-dung made up into cakes. This, indeed, is much used in every part of India, especially by men of rank; as, from the veneration paid the cow, it is considered as by far the most pure substance that can be employed. Every herd of cattle, when at pasture, is attended by women, and these often of high caste, who with their hands gather up the dung and carry it home in baskets. They then form it into cakes, about half an inch thick, and nine inches in diameter, and stick them on the walls to dry. So different indeed are Hindu notions of cleanliness from ours that the walls of their best houses are frequently bedaubed with these cakes; and every morning numerous females, from all parts of the neighborhood, bring for sale into Seringapatam baskets of this fuel. Many females who carry large baskets of cow-dung on their heads are well-dressed and elegantly formed girls."

Smudges. Dried ordure is generally used for smudges, to drive away insects. The Indians of the Great Plains beyond the Missouri burned the "chips" of the buffalo with this object.

Baker reports that the natives of the White Nile "make tumuli of dung which are constantly on fire, fresh fuel being added constantly, to drive away the mosquitoes."

One of the Chinese recipes given by Du Halde's *History of China* is as follows: "When they burn the dung of a camel, the smoke which proceeds from it destroys Gnats and all kinds of vermin."

In *Heart of Africa,* Schweinfurth describes the Shillooks of the west bank of the Nile as "burning heaps of cow-dung to keep off the flies."

Such smudges were employed by the Arabians to kill bed-bugs.

Human and Animal Excreta to Promote the Growth of the Hair and Eradicate Dandruff. For shampooing the hair, urine was the favorite medium among the Eskimo.

Bernardino de Sahagun's *Historia* gives in detail the formula of the preparation applied by the Mexicans for the eradication of dandruff: "Cut the hair close to the root, wash head well with urine, and afterward take amole (soap-weed) and *coixochitl* leaves, and then the kernels of *aguacate* ground up and mixed with the ashes already spoken of (wood ashes from the fire-place), and then rub on black mud with a quantity of the bark mentioned (mesquite)."

According to Hippocrates, dove-dung was also applied externally in the treatment of baldness.

The urine of the foal of an ass was supposed to thicken the hair. Camel's dung, reduced to ashes and mixed with oil, was said to curl and frizzle the hair. Sir Samuel Baker says that the natives of the Nile above Khartoum have "their hair stained red by a plaster of ashes and cow's urine."

And, according to Schweinfurth, the Shillooks of the west bank make "repeated applications of clay, gum, or dung" to their hair.

Schurig says that swallow-dung was of conceded efficacy as a hair-dye, and was applied frequently as an ointment. He recommends the use of mouse-dung for scald head and dandruff, and even to excite the growth of the beard.

For loss of hair, the dung of pigeons, cats, rats, mice, geese, swallows, rabbits, or goats, or human urine, applied externally, were highly recommended by Paullini, in his *Dreck Apothek*.

Cat-dung was highly recommended by Sextus Placitus.

As a Means of Washing Vessels. A personal letter from Chief Engineer Melville (U.S. Navy) states that the natives of Eastern Siberia use urine "for cleansing their culinary materials."

According to Sir Samuel Baker, "The Obbo natives are similar to the Bari in some of their habits. I have had great difficulty in breaking my cow-keeper of his disgusting custom of washing the milk-bowl with cow's urine, and even mixing some with the milk. He declares that unless he washes his hands with such water before milking, the cows will lose their milk. This filthy custom is unaccountable."

In the County Cork, Ireland, rusty tin dishes are scoured with cow manure; the manure is blessed, and so will benefit the dishes and bring good luck. It is not an infrequent custom to bury *keelars* and other dishes for holding milk under a manure-heap during the winter and early spring (when cows are apt to be dry, and the milk-dishes empty), to protect the dishes from persons evilly disposed, who might cast a spell on them, and so bewitch either the cows or the milk. Such an evil-eyed person could not harm a dish unless empty.

Filthy Habits in Cooking. Franz Boas recounts in "The Central Eskimo" that the Eskimo relate stories of a people who preceded them in the Polar regions called the Tornit. Of these predecessors, they say, "Their way of preparing meat was disgusting, since they let it become putrid, and placed it between the thigh and the belly to warm it."

This recalls the similar method of the Tartars, who used to seat themselves on their horses with their meat under them.

15.

TOLLS OF FLATULENCE
EXACTED OF PROSTITUTES

in

FRANCE

N A WORK BY THE ABBÉ ROUBAUD, ENTITLED "LaPéterade" Poem in Four Stanzas, we are informed, "One refers to Ducange's *Glossary* in order to prove that in France one used the fart as a form of monetary exchange in the payment of tolls."

If we may believe Victor Hugo, the custom of the *péage* (toll) at the bridge of Montluc was generally known to the people of France in the fifteenth century. Thus, in the first chapter of *Notre-Dame,* the populace of Paris, at the Feast of Fools, are represented as indulging in much badinage:

"Dr. Claude Choart, are you seeking Marie la Giffards?"
"She's in the Rue de Glatigny."
"She's paying her four deniers–*quatuor denarios.*"
"*Aut unum bumbum.*" ("And one fart.")

Jacques Dulaure again quotes Ducange's *Glossary* in regard to the tolls demanded of public women first crossing the bridge at

Montluc. He finds the description of this peculiar toll in registers dating back to 1398. He also sees the resemblance between this toll and the tenure of the Manor of Essington.

Surgeon Robert M. O'Reilly, U.S. Army, states that among the Irish settlers who came to the United States in the closing hours of the last century the expression was common, in speaking of Flatulence, to term it "Sir-Reverence."

"Sir-Reverence. In old writers, a common corruption of 'save reverence,' or 'saving your reverence,'—an apologetic phrase used when mentioning anything deemed improper or unseemly, and especially a euphemism for *stercus humanum*." This is from Stevens' *Spanish Dictionary* of 1706.

16.

URINE

in

CEREMONIAL
OBSERVANCES

N THE EXAMPLES ADDUCED FROM FREDERICK Whymper's *Alaska* concerning the people of the village of Unlacheet on Norton Sound, "the *dancers* of the Malemutes of Norton Sound bathed themselves in urine." Although, on another page, Whymper says that this was for want of soap, doubt may, with some reason, be entertained. Bathing is a frequent accompaniment, an integral part of the religious ceremonial among all the Indians of America, and no doubt among the Inuit or Eskimo as well. When this is performed by dancers, there is further reason to examine carefully for a religious complication, and especially if these dances be celebrated in sacred places, as Ivan Petroff relates they are. "They never bathe or wash their bodies, but on certain occasions the men light a fire in the *kashima,* strip themselves, and dance and jump around until in a profuse perspiration. They then apply urine to their oily bodies and rub themselves until a lather appears, after which they plunge into the river."

Dr. W. J. Hoffman writes in a personal letter dated June 16, 1890: "The following information received from Victor Namoff, a Kadiack of mixed blood, relates to a ceremonial dance which he observed among the Aiga-lukamut Eskimo of the southern coast of Alaska. The informant, as his father had been before him, had for a number of years been employed by the Russians to visit the various tribes on the mainland to conduct trade for the collection of furs and peltries. Besides being perfectly familiar with the English and Russian languages, he had acquired considerable familiarity with quite a number of native dialects, and was thus enabled to mingle with the various peoples among whom much of his time was spent. The ceremony was conducted in a large partly underground chamber, of oblong shape, having a continuous platform or shelf, constructed so as to be used either as seats or for sleeping. The only light obtained was from native oil lamps. The participants, numbering about ten dozen, were entirely naked, and after being seated a short time, several natives, detailed as musicians, began to sing. Then one of the natives arose, and performed the disgusting operation of urinating over the back and shoulders of the person seated next him, after which he jumped down upon the ground, and began to dance, keeping time with the music. The one who had been subjected to the operation just mentioned, then subjected his nearest neighbor to a similar douche, and he in turn the next in order, and so on until the last person on the bench had been similarly dealt with, he in turn being obliged to accommodate the initiator of the movement, who ceases dancing for that purpose. In the meantime, all those who have relieved themselves step down and join in the dance, which is furious and violent, inducing great perspiration and an intolerable stench. No additional information was given further than that the structure may have been used in this instance as a sudatory, the urine and violent movements being deemed sufficient to supply the necessary amount of moisture and heat to supply the participants with a sweat-bath."

In *Our Arctic Province*, Henry Elliott describes the "Orgies" in the *kashgas*, as he styles them. "The fire is usually drawn from the hot stones on the hearth. A *kantog* of chamber-lye poured over them, which, rising in dense clouds of vapor, gives notice by its presence and its horrible ammoniacal odor to the delighted inmates that the bath is on. The *kashga* is heated to suffocation; it is full of smoke and the outside men run in from their huts with wisps of dry grass for towels and bunches of alder twigs to flog their naked bodies."

He continues, "They throw off their garments; they shout and dance and whip themselves into profuse perspiration as they caper in the hot vapor. More of their disgusting substitute for soap is rubbed on, and produces a lather, which they rub off with cold water. This is the most enjoyable occasion of an Indian's existence, as he solemnly affirms. Nothing else affords a tithe of infinite pleasure which this orgy gives him. To us, however, there is nothing about him so offensive as that stench which such a performance arouses."

In the Bareshnun ceremony, Dosabhai Framje Karaka says in *The History of the Parsees* that the Parsee priest "has to undergo certain ablutions wherein he has to apply to his body cow's urine, and sand and clay, which seem to have been the common and cheapest disinfectant known to the ancient Iranians."

Captain Henri Jouan of the French Navy writes in a personal letter: "In 1847, I was then twenty-six years old, once an old woman (in Cherbourg) came to me with a washing-pan, and asked me to piss into it, as the urine of a stout healthy young man was required to wash the bosoms of a young woman who was just delivered of a child."

In Scotland, the breasts of a young mother were washed with salt and water to ensure a good flow of milk. The practice is alluded to in the following couplet from *The Fortunate Shepherdess* by Alexander Ross, 1778.

> *Jean's paps with salt and water washen clean,*
> *Reed that her milk get wrang, fen it was green.*

This practice seems closely allied to the one immediately preceding. We shall have occasion to show that salt and water, holy water, and other liquids superseded human urine in several localities, Scotland among others.

In the *Private Journal of H.M.S. Hecla*, G. F. Lyon says this about the Central Eskimo: "A few days after birth, or according to the fancy of the parents, an *angekok*, who by relationship or long acquaintance with the family, has attained terms of great friendship, makes use of some vessel and with the urine of the mother washes the infant while all the gossips around pour forth their good wishes for the little one to prove an active man, if a boy, or, if a girl, the mother of plenty of children. The ceremony, I believe is never omitted, and is called *Gogsinariva*." The same custom is practiced by the Eskimo of Cumberland Sound.

The following comes from George Turner's *Samoa*: "The drinking of the water in which a new-born babe had been bathed is intimated in the myths of the Samoans. When the first baby was born, 'Salevao provided water for washing the child, and made it *Saor*, sacred to Moa. The rocks and the earth said they wished to get some of that water to drink. Salevao replied that if they got a bamboo he would send them a streamlet through it, and hence the origin of springs.' " Although it is not so stated in the text, yet from analogy with other cosmogonies, we may entertain a suspicion as to how the god provided the water–no doubt from his own person.

17.

ORDURE

in

SMOKING

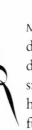

MONG ALL THE OBSERVANCES OF THE EVERY-day life of the American aborigine, none is so distinctly complicated with the religious idea as smoking; therefore, should the use of excrement, human or animal be detected in this connection, full play should be given to the suspicion that a hidden meaning attaches to the ceremony. This would appear to be the view entertained in *Oregon Missions* by the indefatigable missionary, Father De Smet, who records such a custom among the Flatheads and Crows in 1846: "To render the odor of the pacific incense agreeable to their gods, it is necessary that the tobacco and the herb (*skwiltz*), the usual ingredients, should be mixed with a small quantity of buffalo dung."

The Sioux, Cheyennes, Arapahoes, and others of the plains tribes, to whom the buffalo is a god, have the same or an almost similar custom.

According to Thurnberg's *Account of the Cape of Good Hope,* the

Hottentots, when in want of tobacco, "smoke the dung of the two-horned rhinoceros or of elephants."

The followers of the Grand Lama, as already noted, make use of his dried excrements as snuff, and an analogous employment of the dried dung of swine retained a place in the medical practice of Europe until the beginning of the present century, and many, perhaps, still survive in the folk-medicine of isolated villages.

According to Pliny, the people of Achaia say "that the smoke of dried cow dung, that of the animal when grazing I mean, is remarkably good for phthisis, when inhaled through a reed."

Dung is also used in Central Africa. Chaille Long reports, "A huge bowl is filled with tobacco and clay and sometimes with a questionable mixture, the fumes are inhaled until the smoker falls stupified or deadly sick—this effect alone being sought for."

W. W. Rockhill writes in a personal letter: "In Algeria, gazelle droppings are put in snuff and smoking tobacco; the Mongol Tartars mix the ashes of yak manure with their snuff."

Mr. Rudyard Kipling shows in his *Plain Tales from the Hills* that the native population of India is accustomed to use a mixture of one part of tobacco to three of cow-dung.

18.

COURTSHIP

and

MARRIAGE

"TO MULTIPLY AND REPLENISH THE EARTH" was the first command given to man. To love, and to desire to be loved in return, is the strongest impulse of our nature, and therefore it need surprise no student who sets about investigating the occult properties attributed to the human and animal egestae to find them in very general use in the composition of love-philters, as antidotes to such philters, as aphrodisiacs, as antiphrodisiacs, and as aids to delivery. Human ordure was in constant use in the manufacture of these philters, being administered both internally and externally. On this point it may be proper to cite Schurig, who explains that it was sometimes put in porridge, and in other cases in the shoes.

Johannes Frommann gives an instance of a woman who made love-philters out of her own excrement in his *Tractatus de Fascinatione* (1675). As late as Frommann's day, the use of such philters was punishable with death. The remedies for love-philters were composed of human skull, coral, verbena flowers, secundines, or after-birth, and a copious flow of urine. He says that Paracelsus taught that when one person ate or drank anything given off by the skin of another, he would fall desperately in love with that other. He also cites Daniel Beckherius to the effect that some philters were made of perspiration, menses, or semen.

Pliny recommends "the urine that has been voided by a bull immediately after covering taken in drink," as an aphrodisiac; and "the groin well rubbed with earth moistened with this urine."

According to Sextus Placitus, an ointment of the gall of goats, incense, goat-dung, and nettle-seeds was applied to the privy parts previous to copulation to increase the amorousness of women.

Martin Schurig reports that leopard-dung was in repute as an aphrodisiac.

Samuel Flemming tells us that we should not pass over in silence the fact that human seed has been employed by some persons as medicine. They believed that its magnetic power could be used in philters, and that by it a lover could feed the flame of his mistress's affections; hence from it was prepared what was known as "magnetic mummy," which, being given to a woman, threw her into an inextinguishable frenzy of love for the man or animal yielding it. Others credited it with a wonderful efficacy in relieving inveterate epilepsy, or restoring virility impaired by incantation or witchcraft; for which purpose it was used while still fresh, before exposure to the air, in pottage, mixed with the powder of mace. In *De Remediis* (1738), Flemming alludes to a horrible use of relics, good and bad, upon which human semen had been ejaculated; but this involved so much of the grossest impiety that he declined to enter into full details.

The love-philter described in the preceding paragraph recalls a somewhat analogous practice among the Manicheans, whose eucharistic bread was incorporated or sprinkled with human semen, possibly with the idea that the bread of life should be sprinkled with the life-giving excretion. The Albigenses, or Catharistes, their descendants, are alleged to have degenerated into or preserved the same vile superstition.

According to Brand's *Popular Antiquities,* the method of divination by which maidens strove to rekindle the expiring flames of affection in the hearts of husbands and lovers by making cake from dough kneaded on the woman's posterior seems to have held on in England as a game among little girls, in which one lies down on the floor, on her back, rolling backwards and forwards, and repeating the following lines:

Cockledy bread, mistley cake
When you do that for our sake.

While one of the party so lay down, the rest of the party sat round. They lay down and rolled in this manner by turns.

These words "mistley" and "cockledy" were not to be found in any of the lexicons examined, or in the *Dictionary of Obsolete and Provincial English* of Thomas Wright (London, 1869), although in the last was the word "mizzly," meaning "mouldy."

Muhongo, an African boy from Angola, relates the following: "When a young man is trying to win the love of a reluctant girl he consults the medicine-man, who then tries to find some of the urine and saliva which the girl has voided, as well as the sand upon which it has fallen. He mixes these with a few twigs of certain woods, and places them in a gourd, and gives them to the young man, who takes them home, and adds a portion of tobacco. In about an hour he takes out the tobacco and gives it to the girl to smoke. This effects a complete transformation in her feelings."

To protect the population from the baleful effects of the love-philter, there was, fortunately, the anti-philter, in which, strangely enough, we come upon some of the same ingredients. Thus mouse-dung, applied in "the form of a liniment, acts as an anti-phrodisiac," according to Pliny. Or: "A lizard drowned in urine has the effect of an antiphrodisiac upon the man whose urine it is."

Pliny also states, "According to Osthanes, a woman will forget her former love by taking a he-goat's urine in drink."

A journeyman cabinet-maker had been given a love-potion by a young woman so that he couldn't keep away from her. His mother then bought a pair of new shoes for him, put into them certain herbs, and in them he had to run to a certain town. A can of urine was then put into his right shoe, out of which he drank, whereupon he perfectly despised the object of his former affection.

According to Paullini, a man was given in his food some of the dried ordure of a woman whom he formerly loved, and that created a terrible antipathy toward her.

Likewise, to break up a love affair, nothing was superior to the simple charm of placing some of the ordure of the person seeking to break away from love's thraldom in the shoe of the one still faithful. Schurig reports how a prostitute gave a love-potion to a captain in the army. Some of her ordure was placed in a new shoe, and after he had walked therein an hour, and had his fill of the smell, the spell was broken.

Mr. Chrisfield of the Library of Congress in Washington, D.C. imparts a fact which dovetails in with the foregoing item in a very interesting manner. He says that, in his youth, which was passed on the Eastern Shore of Maryland, he learned that among the more ignorant classes of that section it was a rule that when a father observed the growing affection of his son for some young girl, he should endeavor to obtain a little of her excrement, and make the youth wear it under the left arm-pit. If he remained constant in his devotion after being subject to this test, the father felt that it would be useless to interpose objection to the nuptials.

According to Reginald Scot's *Discoverie of Witchcraft*, "To procure the dissolving of bewitched and constrained love, the party bewitched must make a jakes (i.e., privy) of the lover's shoe. And to enforce a man, how proper soever he be, to love an old hag, she gives unto him to eate (among other meates) her own dung."

19.

INITIATION

of

WARRIORS

–

CONFIRMATION

HE ATTAINMENT BY YOUNG MEN OF THE AGE OF manhood is an event which among all primitive peoples has been signalized by peculiar ceremonies. In a number of instances ordure and urine have been employed, as for example: The observances connected with this event in the lives of Australian warriors are kept a profound secret, but, among the few learned is the fact that the neophyte is "plastered with goat dung."

In some parts of Australia, Brough Smyth says in *Aborigines of Australia* that the youth of fourteen or fifteen had to submit himself to the rite of *Tid-but,* during which his head was shaved and plastered with mud "and his body is daubed with clay, mud, and charcoal-powder and filth of every kind." (Smyth had previously specified goat-dung.) "He carries a basket under his arm, containing moist clay, charcoal, and filth. He gathers filth as he goes, and places it in the basket." The young initiate throws his filth at all the men he meets, but not at the women or children, as these have been warned to keep out of his way. It is surely remarkable to stumble upon the counterpart of one of the proceedings of the Feast of Fools in such a remote corner of the globe.

John Frazer expounds in a personal letter: "One observer of the customs of the blacks has stated in the journal of the Anthropological Society of London that in the Hunter River District of New South Wales, the catechumens at some parts of the *Bora* ceremonies are required to eat ordure. I have made diligent inquiries in the same locality and elsewhere, but have found nothing to corroborate his statement. Similarly, in one district in Queensland, it is said that the blacks, whether at the *Bora* or not I cannot say, make cup-like holes in the clay soil, collect their urine in them, and drink it afterwards. This latter statement may be true, but I have never been able to substantiate it by information from those who know. Various considerations, however, lead me to think it possible that our blacks, in some places at least (for their observances are not everywhere the same), may use ordure and urine in that way, thinking that the evil spirit will be propitiated by their eating in his honor that which he himself delights to eat; just as in Northwestern India a devotee may be seen going about with his body plastered all over with human dung in honor of his god. And our blacks have good reason to try to propitiate this unclean spirit (Gunung-dhukhya) in every possible way, for they believe that he can enter their bodies, and effecting a lodgment in their abdomen, feed there on the foulest of the contents, and thus cause cramps, fits, madness, and other serious disorders."

This correspondent has struck the keynote of the curious behavior of the prophet Ezekiel and others. Believing, as was believed in their day, that deities ate excrement, why should not they, the representatives of the gods, eat it too? And if a god enter into a man's body to eat excrement, why should not the victim feed him on that which is so acceptable, and by gorging him free himself from pain?

In "The Ethnography of the Western Tribes of Torres Straits," A. C. Haddon offers the following: "In order to infuse courage into boys, a warrior, *Kerketegerkai,* would take the eye and the tongue of a dead man (probably of a slain enemy), and after mincing them and mixing with his urine, would administer the compound in the following manner. He would tell the boy to shut his eyes and not look, adding: 'I give you proper *kaikai*' (*Kaikai* is an introduced word, being the jargon English for food.) The warrior then stood up behind the sitting youth, and putting the latter's hand between his (the man's) legs, would feed him. After this dose, 'heart along, boy no fright.' "

Monier Williams reports in *Modern India* that a young Parsi undergoes a sort of confirmation, during which "he is made to drink a small quantity of the urine of a bull."

A religious rite of still more fearful import occurs among the Hottentots at the initiation of their young men into the ranks of warriors–a ceremony which must be deferred until the postulant has attained his eighth or ninth year. It consists, principally, in depriving him of the left testicle, after which the medicine man voids his urine upon him.

In *Voyage to the Cape of Good Hope,* Kolbein describes it as follows: "At eight or nine years of age, the young Hottentot is, with great ceremony, deprived of his left testicle." He says nothing about an aspersion with urine in this instance, but on the succeeding page he narrates that there is first a sermon from one of the old men, who afterwards "evacuates a smoking stream of urine all over him, having before reserved his water for that purpose. The youth receives the stream with eagerness and joy; and making furrows with the long nails in the fat upon his body, rubs in briny fluid with the quickest action. The old man, having given him the last drop, utters aloud the following benediction: 'Good fortune attend thee. Live to old age. Increase and multiply. May thy beard grow soon.' "

Kolbein continues, "The young Hottentot, who has won the reputation of a hero by killing a lion, tiger, leopard, elephant, etc., is entitled to wear a bladder in his hair. He is formally congratulated by all his kraal. One of the medicine-men marches up to the hero and pours a plentiful stream over him from head to foot—pronouncing over him certain terms which I could never get explained. The hero, as in other cases, rubs in the smoking stream upon his face and every other part with the greatest eagerness."

The Indians of California gave urine to newly-born children. H. H. Bancroft relates in *Native Races of the Pacific Slope,* "At time of childbirth, many singular observances obtained. For instance, the old women washed the child as soon as it was born, and drank of the water. The unhappy infant was forced to take a draught of urine medicinally."

According to Henry Rink's *Tales and Traditions of the Eskimo,* in order to bring up an Eskimo child to be an *Angerd-lartug-sick,* that is, "a man brought up in a peculiar manner, with a view to acquiring a certain faculty by means of which he might be called to life again and returned to land, in case he should be drowned, the mother had to keep a strict fast and the child to be accustomed to the smell of urine."

In a personal letter, Reverend H. K. Trumbull offers this explanation: "I am strongly inclined to the belief that all these rites are survivals or debased vestiges of the blood-covenant practice, by which the partaking of each other's selves is a form of covenanting by which two persons become as one. Are you aware of the fact that the habit of giving the urine of a healthy child to a new-born babe has prevailed down to the present day among rustic nurses in New England, if not elsewhere, in America? I can bear personal testimony to this fact from absolute knowledge. It is a noteworthy fact that the Hebrew word *chaneek*, which is translated 'trained' or 'initiated,' and which is used in the proverb, 'Train up a child,' etc., has as its root-idea (as shown in the corresponding Arabic word) the 'opening of the gullet' in a new-born child, starting the child in its new life. Among some primitive peoples, fresh blood, as added life, is thus given to a babe; and in other cases it is urine."

J. G. Forlong in *Rivers of Life* states that at the time of investiture of the Indian boy with the sacred thread, "the fire is kindled with the droppings of the sacred cow."

20.

HUNTING

and

FISHING

CCORDING TO FATHER MEROLLA IN *VOYAGE TO Congo,* the African hunter in pursuit of game, such as elephants, anoints himself "all over with their dung." This, he says, is merely to deceive the animal with the smell.

Muhongo reports that the people of Angola, when about to set out on a hunt, are careful to collect the dung of the elephant, antelope, and other kinds of wild animals, and hand them to the medicine-man, who makes a magical compound out of them, and places it in a horn. It then serves as an amulet, and will ensure success in the hunt.

Pliny relates that in Heraklea the country-people poisoned panthers with aconite. But the panthers had sense enough to know that human excrement was an antidote. In Book VIII, Chapter 41, he tells of the aconite-poisoned panther curing itself by eating human excrement. Knowing this fact, the peasants suspend human excrement in a pot so high in the air that the panther exhausts itself in jumping to reach it, and dies all the sooner.

The reindeer Tchuktchi feign to be passing urine in order to catch their animals which they want to use with their sleds. The reindeer, horses, and cattle of the Siberian tribes are very fond of urine, probably on account of the salt it contains, and when they see a man walking out from the hut, as if for the purpose of relieving his bladder, they follow him up close, and so closely that he finds the operation anything but pleasant.

The Arctic explorer W. H. Gilder writes in a personal letter: "The Esquimaux of King William's Land and the adjacent peninsula often catch the wild reindeer by digging a pit in the deep snow, and covering it with thin blocks of snow, that would break with the weight of an animal. They then make a line of urine from several directions leading to the center of the cover of the pitfall, where an accumulation of snow, saturated with the urine of the dog, is deposited as bait. One or more animals are thereby led to their destruction."

He continues, "The dogs of the Esquimaux are equally fond of excrement, especially in cold weather, and when a resident of the Arctic desires to relieve himself, he finds it necessary to take a whip or a stick to defend himself against the energy of the hungry dogs. Often, when a man wants to urge his dog-team to greater exertion, he sends his wife or one of the boys to run ahead, and when at a distance, to stoop down and make believe he is relieving himself. The dogs are thus spurred to furious exertion, and the boy runs on again, to repeat the delusion. This never fails of the desired effect, no matter how often repeated."

In "The Maoris of New Zealand," E. Tregaar states: "I only know one superstitious use of excrement–that wherein the hooks were placed round some before the fishing incantations began."

21.

ORDEALS

and

PUNISHMENTS,

TERRESTRIAL

and

SUPERNAL

HE CHINESE HAVE A VERY CURIOUS AND VERY horrible mode of punishment. Criminals of certain classes are enclosed in barrels or boxes filled with building lime, and exposed in a public street to the rays of the noon-day sun. Food in plenty is within reach of the unfortunate wretches, but it is salt fish, or other salt provision, with all the water needed to satisfy the thirst this food is certain to excite, but in the very alleviation of which the poor criminals are only adding to the torments to overtake them when by a more copious discharge from the kidneys the lime shall "quicken" and burn them to death.

According to the *Adventures of Andrew Battell* in Loango, Africa, "When a man is suspected of an offence he is carried before the king," and "is compelled to drink an infusion of a kind of root called *imbando*. The virtue of this root is that, if they put too much into the water, the person that drinketh it cannot void urine. The ordeal consists in drinking and then in urinating as a proof of innocence."

In Sierra Leone, the natives have a curious custom to which they subject all of their tribe suspected of poisoning. Lieutenant John Matthews reports in his *Voyage* that they make the culprit drink a certain "red water; after which for twenty-four hours he is not allowed to ease nature by any evacuation; and should he not be able to restrain them, it would be considered as strong a proof of his guilt as if he had fallen a victim to the first draught."

Herodotus relates that Pheron, the son of Sesostris, conqueror of Egypt, became blind, and remained so for ten years. "But in the eleventh year an oracle reached him from the city of Buto, importing that the time of his punishment was expired, and he should recover his sight by washing his eyes with the urine of a woman who had intercourse with her own husband only, and had known no other man." Herodotus goes on to relate that Pheron tried the urine of his own wife and that of many other women ineffectually. Finally, he was cured by the urine of a woman whom he took to wife. All the others he burnt to death.

"Fasting on bread and drinking water defiled by the excrement of a fowl" are among the disciplinary punishments cited in Fosbroke's *Monachism*. This specimen of monastic discipline may be better understood when read between the lines. The veneration surrounding chicken-dung in the religious system of the Celts, prior to the introduction of the Christian religion, could be uprooted in no more complete manner than by making its use a matter of scorn and contempt. History is replete with examples wherein we are taught that the things which are held most sacred in one cult are the very ones upon which the fury and scorn of the superceding cultus are wreaked.

In several parts of Germany, the Fool of the Carnival was buried under a dung-heap. Further on, is given this explanation in J. G. Frazer's *The Golden Bough*: "The burying of the representative of the Carnival under a dung-heap is natural, if he is supposed to possess a quickening and fertilizing influence like that ascribed to the effigy of Death."

Frazer continues by relating the following practices: "In Siam, it was formerly the custom on one day of the year to single out a woman broken down by debauchery, and carry her on a litter through all the streets to the music of drums and hautboys. The mob insulted her and pelted her with dirt; and, after having carried her through the whole city, they threw her on a dunghill. They believed that the woman thus drew upon herself all the malign influences of the air and of evil spirits."

In Swabia, there is a rough harvest game in which one of the laborers takes the part of the sow. He is pursued by his comrades and if they catch him "they handle him roughly, beating him, blackening or dirtying his face, throwing him into filth. At other times he is put in a wheelbarrow. After being wheeled round the village, he is flung on a dunghill."

"The Iroquois inaugurated the new year in January with a festival of dreams. It was a time of general license. Many seized the opportunity of paying off old scores by belaboring obnoxious persons, covering them with filth and hot ashes."

"During the madder harvest in the Dutch province of Zealand, a stranger passing by a field where the people are digging the madder roots 'will sometimes call out to them, *Koortspillers'* (a term of reproach). Upon this, two of the fleetest runners make after him, and if they catch him, they bring him back to the madder field and bury him in the earth up to his middle at least, jeering at him all the while. They then ease nature before his face."

"Now, it is an old superstition that by easing nature on the spot where a robbery is committed, the robbers secure themselves for a certain time against interruption. The fact, therefore, that the madder-diggers resort to this proceeding in presence of the stranger proves that they consider themselves robbers and the stranger as the person robbed."

The Negroes of Guinea are firm believers in the theory of Obsession, and have a god Abiku who, according to Baudin's *Fetichism,* "takes up his abode in the human body." He generally bothers little children, who sometimes die. "If the child dies, the body is thrown on the dirt-heap to be devoured by wild beasts."

In connection with the above, the following from Francis Grose's *Dictionary of Buckish Slang* deserves consideration: "Reverence. An ancient custom which obliges any person easing himself near the highway or footpath, on the word 'reverence' being given him by a passenger, to take off his hat with his teeth, and, without moving from his station, to throw it over his head, by which it frequently falls in the excrement. This was considered as a punishment for the breach of delicacy. A person refusing to obey this law might be pushed backwards. Hence, perhaps, the term 'sir reverence.' "

Robert Southey's *Commonplace Book* says that "the ducking stool was a legal punishment. Roguish brewers and bakers were also liable to it, and they were to be ducked in *stercore* in the town ditch." He also states that, in the Hindu mythology, "slanderers and calumniators, stretched upon beds of red-hot iron, shall be obliged to eat excrements."

According to the *Vasishtha,* among the unlawful acts for Brahmans or Kshatriyas who are compelled to support themselves by following the occupations of Vaisyas, is selling sesamum, unless "they themselves have produced it by tillage. If he applies sesamum to any other purpose but food, anointing, and charitable gifts, he will be born again as a worm, and together with his ancestors be plunged into his own ordure."

David Crantz reports in *History of Greenland*: "Forbearance from meat and work are also prescribed to a single woman in case the sun or moon (though we should rather call it a bird flying by) should let any uncleanness drop upon her. Otherwise, she might be unfortunate, or even deprived of her life."

The Australians believed that if a man did not allow the septum of the nose to be pierced, he would suffer in the next world. In *Aborigines of Victoria,* Smyth says, "As soon as ever the spirit Egowk left the body, it would be required, as a punishment, to eat *Toorta-gwannang* (filth not proper for translation)." With this, compare the declaration of the Indian *Manes* that a Kahatya who has not done his duty, will, after death, have to live on ordure and carrion.

The Hebrew prophets sat on dungheaps while the recalcitrant

people of Israel were warned: "Behold, I will spread dung upon your faces, even the dung of your solemn feasts, and one shall take you away with it" (Malachi, II, 3).

The historian Suetonius relates that the unfortunate Roman emperor Vitellius was pelted with excrement before being put to death.

22.

INSULTS

NIEBUHR SAYS IN *DESCRIPTION DE L'ARABIE* that the grossest insult that can be offered to a man, especially a Mahometan in Arabia, is to spit upon his beard, or to say "*De l'ordure sur ta barbe.*" In *Arabian Nights,* Burton remarks, "*Khara,* meaning dung, is the lowest possible insult. *Ta-kara* is the commonest of insults, used also by modest women. I have heard a mother use it to her son."

In Angola, Africa, the greatest insult is, "Go and eat s——t." According to Muhongo, flatulence is freely permitted among the natives; but any license of this kind taken while strangers are in the vicinity is regarded as a deadly insult.

In the report of one of the early American explorations to the Trans-Missouri region (*Long's Expedition*) occurs the story that the Republican Pawnees, Nebraska, once (about 1780–90) violated the laws of hospitality by seizing a calumet-bearer of the Omahas who had entered their village, and, among other indignities, making him "drink urine mixed with bison gall."

It is somewhat singular to find in the myths of the Zuñis–the very people among whom we have discovered the existence of this filthy rite of urine-drinking–an allusion to the fact that to throw urine upon persons or near their dwellings was to be looked upon as an insult of the gravest character. During the early winter of 1881 the author was at the Pueblo of Zuñi, New Mexico, while Mr. Frank H. Cushing was engaged in the researches which have since placed him at the head of American anthropologists, and then heard recited by the old men the long myth of the young boy who went to the Spirit Land to seek his father. One of the incidents upon which the story-tellers dwelt with much insistence was the degradation and ignominy in which the boy and his poor mother lived in their native village, as was shown by the fact that their neighbors were in the habit of emptying their urine vessels upon their roof and in front of their door.

The expression "excrement eater" is applied by the Mandans and others on the Upper Missouri as a term of the vilest opprobrium, according to Surgeon Washington Matthews (U.S. Army).

Among the Cheyenne expressions of contempt is to be found one which recalls the objurgations of the Bedouins; namely, *natsiviz,* or "s——t-mouth."

Reverend J. Owen Dorsey, who has made such prolonged and careful studies of the manners and myths of the tribes of the Siouan stock, is authority for the statement that the worst insult that one Ponca can give to another is to say, "You are an eater of dog-dung." And it is noticeable that the words of the expression are rarely used in the language of every-day life.

According to Steller, the Kamchatkans say, "May you have one hundred burning lamps in your podex" and "Eater of feces with his fish-spawn."

George Smith quotes from *The Chaldean Account of Genesis*: "May the garbage of the foundations of the city be thy food. May the drains of the city be thy drink."

The dispute between Richard the Lion-Hearted and the Arch-Duke of Austria, which resulted afterwards in the incarceration of the English king in a dungeon, had its rise in the great insult of throwing the Austrian standard down into a privy. Matthew of Paris says distinctly that Richard himself did this. "Now he, being over well disposed to the cause of the Norman, waxed wroth with the Duke's train, and gave a headstrong, unseemly order for the Duke's banner to be cast into a cesspool."

Readers of classical history will recall the incident of the outrage perpetrated by the mob of Tarentum upon the person of the Roman ambassador Posthumus in 282 B.C. A buffoon in the street threw filth upon his toga. The ambassador refused to be mollified, and tersely telling his assailants that many a drop of Tarentine blood would be required to wash out the stains, took his departure. A cruel war followed, and the Tarentines were reduced to the rank of a conquered province.

"When the multitude had come to Jerusalem, to the feast of unleavened bread, and the Roman cohort stood over the temple, one of the soldiers pulled back his garment, and stooping down after an indecent manner, turned his posteriors to the Jews, and spake such words as might be expected upon such a posture." The narration of Josephus in *Wars of the Jews* describes the riot which followed as a result, and ten thousand people were killed.

The threat made against the Jews in the Old Testament deserves consideration in this connection, "There shall not be left one that pisses against the wall."

The Emperor Caracalla put to death those who made water in front of his statues.

Grose's *Dictionary of Slang* reports that among the rough games of English sailors was one, "The Galley," in which a mopful of excrement was thrust in a landsman's face.

> "The devil's dung in thy teeth."
> Thomas Dekkas, *The Honest Whore* (1604)

23.

Mortuary
Ceremonies

N THE CREMATION OF A HINDU CORPSE AT Bombay, the ashes of the pyre were sprinkled with water, a cake of cow-dung placed in the center, and around it a small stream of cow-urine. Upon this were placed plantain-leaves, rice cakes, and flowers.

According to De Gubernatis' *Zoological Mythology,* "They who return from the funeral must touch the stone of Priapus, a fire, the excrement of a cow, a grain of sesame, and water–all symbols of that fecundity which the contact with a corpse might be destroyed."

A Parsee is defiled by touching a corpse. According to the *Shapast la Shayast,* "And when he is in contact and does not move it, he is to be washed with bull's urine and water."

In the *Zendavesta,* it says that if the clothing of the dead "has not been defiled with seed or sweat or dirt or vomit, then the worshippers of Mazda shall wash it with gomez." Gomez or bull-urine was alluded to as the great purifier. The sacred vessels that had been defiled by the touch of a corpse were to be cleaned with gomez. The most efficacious gomez was that of an "ungelded bull."

"Let the worshippers of Mazda here bring the urine wherewith the corpse-bearers shall wash their hair and their bodies."

In addition, it says that "they shall cover the surface of the grave with ashes or cow-dung."

In describing the funerals of the Eskimo in *Schwatka's Search*, W. H. Gilder says: "The closing of the ceremony was a most touching one. After 'Papa' had returned from the grave, Armow went out of doors and brought in a piece of frozen something that is not polite to specify, further than that the dogs had entirely done with it, and with it he touched every block of snow on a level with the beds of the igloo. The article was then taken out of doors and tossed up in the air, to fall at his feet; and by the manner in which it fell he could joyfully announce that there was no liability of further deaths in camp for some time to come."

Franz Boas gives this account in "The Central Eskimo": "When a child dies, women who carried it in their hands must throw their jackets away if the child has urinated on them. This is part of the custom that everything that has come in contact with a dead person must be destroyed."

There is also a purification of the soul of the dying by the same peculiar methods. In Coromandel, the dying man is so placed that his face will come under the tail of a cow. The tail is lifted, and the cow excited to void her urine. If the urine fall on the face of the sick man, the people cry out with joy, considering him to be one of the blessed; but if the sacred animal be in no humor to gratify their wishes, they are greatly afflicted.

With equal solicitude does the Hottentot medicine-man follow the remains of his kinsmen to the grave, aspersing with the same sacred liquid the corpse of the dead and the persons of the mourners who bewail his fate.

In *Voyage to the Cape of Good Hope,* Kolbein says that at Hottentot funerals, "two old men, the friends or relations of the deceased, enter each circle and sparingly dispense their streams upon each person, so that all may have some. All of the company receive their water with eagerness and veneration. This being done, each steps into the hut, and taking up a handful of ashes from the hearth, comes out by the passage made by the corpse, and strews the ashes by little and little upon the whole company. This, they say, is done to humble their pride."

Brough Smyth reports in *Aborigines of Victoria*: "It is a pity that men in a savage state should take delight in doing that which is nasty, but such is the fact. It is a very common custom for the tribe, or that portion of it who are related to the one who has died, to rub themselves with the moisture that comes from the dead friend. They rub themselves with it until the whole of them have the same smell as the corpse." But, in a footnote, he adds that some of the Australians will not touch a dead body with the naked hand.

In the mortuary ceremonies of the Encounter Bay tribe (South Australians), "the old women put human excrement on their heads–the sign of deepest mourning."

According to *Native Tribes of South Australia,* the corpse of an

Australian chief was surrounded "with wailing women, smeared with filth and ashes."

John F. Mann writes in a personal letter from New South Wales: "In the burial ceremonies, the women of many tribes besmear or plaster their heads with excrement and pipe-clay."

In the Tonga Islands, there are two principal personages–Tooitonga and Veachi–who are believed to be the living representatives of powerful gods. Upon the death of Tooitonga, certain ceremonies are practised, among which: "The men now approach the mount, i.e., the funeral mound, it being dark, and, if the phrase be allowable, perform the devotions to Cloacina, after which they retire. As soon as it is daylight the following morning, the women of the first rank, wives and daughters of the greatest chiefs, assemble with their female attendants, bringing baskets, one holding one side and one the other, advancing two and two, with large shells to clear up the depositions of the preceding night, and in this ceremonious act of humiliation, no female of the highest consequence refuses to take her part. Some of the mourners in the *fytoca* generally come out to assist; so that, in a very little while, the place is made perfectly clean. This is repeated the fourteen following nights, and as punctually cleaned away by sunrise every morning. No persons but the agents are allowed to be witnesses of these extraordinary ceremonies; at least, it would be considered highly indecorous and irreligious to be so. On the sixteenth day, early in the morning, the same females again assemble; but now they are dressed up in the finest *gnatoo*, and most beautiful Hamao mats, decorated with ribbons, and with wreaths of flowers round their necks. They also bring new baskets ornamented with flowers and little brooms, very tastefully made. Thus equipped they approach, and act as if they had the same task to do as before, pretending to clear away the dirt, though no dirt is now there, and take it away in their blankets. The natives themselves used to regret that the filthy part of these ceremonies was necessary to be performed, and that it was the duty of the most exalted nobles, even of the most delicate females of rank, to perform the meanest and most disgusting offices, rather than that the sacred grounds in which he was buried should remain polluted." Peter Dillon says further in *Expedition in Search of La Perouse* that this "must be considered a religious rite, standing upon the foundation of very ancient customs."

24.

MYTHS

HE NAME OF THE CITY OF CHICAGO HAS BEEN
traced by some philologist to the Indian word for
skunk. The urine of this little animal was believed
by some of the Indian tribes to be capable of blind-
ing the man in whose eyes it entered; the animal
itself was deified by the Aztecs under the name of
Tezcatlipoca.

The Apaches have a myth, or story, the analogue of the "Fee-
fo-Fum" of our own childhood; but the giant, instead of smelling
the blood of an Englishman, in the words given in Spanish, "*huele
la cagada*" ("smells excrement").

In the story told by the Kalmucks and Mongols in De Gubernatis' *Zoological Mythology,* "it is under the excrement of a cow that
the enchanted gem, lost by the daughter of the king, is found."

In the mythic lore of the Hindus, the god Utanka sets out on a
journey, protected by Indras. "On his way, he meets a gigantic
bull, and a horseman who bids him, if he would succeed, eat the

excrement of the bull; he does so, rinsing his mouth afterwards." Further on, we learn that Utanka was told "the excrement of the bull was the ambrosia which made him immortal in the kingdom of the serpents."

Ambergris was anciently supposed in Africa to be the dung of the whale or other monster of the sea. This view about the origin of amber was not credited by Avicenna.

Speaking of the *Aidowedo*, the serpent in the Rainbow as believed by the Negroes of Guinea, Father Baudin's *Fetichism* says: "He who finds the excrement of this serpent is rich forever, for with this talisman he can change grains of corn into shells which pass for money." He goes on to narrate a very amusing tale to the effect that the Negroes got the idea that a prism in his possession gave him the power to bring the Rainbow down into his room at will, and that he could obtain unlimited quantities of the precious excrement.

Among some of the Eskimo tribes the Raven is represented as talking to its own excrement and consulting it. Excrement occurs frequently among their legends. From the preceding, we see that the Eskimo must have formerly, even if they do not now, consulted excrement in their divination.

According to George Steller's *Kamtchatka,* there is a riddle among the Kamtchatkans in regard to human feces: "My father has numerous forms and dresses; my mother is warm and thin and bears every day. Before I am born, I like cold and warmth, but after I am born, only cold. In the cold I am strong, and in the warmth, weak; if cold, I am seen far; if warm, I am smelled far."

The people of Kamtchatka believed that rain was the urine of the Billutschi, one of their gods, and of his genii; but after this god has urinated enough, he puts on a new dress made in the form of a sack, and provided with fringes of red seal hair, and variously colored strips of leather. These represent the origin of the Rainbow.

The Kamtchatkan god Kutka was once pursued by enemies, but saved himself "by ejecting from his bowels all kinds of berries, which detained his pursuers."

Another myth of the foolish god Kutka represents him as falling in love with his own excrement and wooing it as his bride. He takes it home in his sleigh, puts it in his bed, and is only restored to a sense of his absurd position by the vile smell.

The myths of the Kamtchatkans offer a parallel to the stories that the presents of the devil always turned into dross. There is the story of the god Kutka, upon whom, as we have seen, many tricks were played. In one, the food with which he supplied himself "turned into past, rotten wood, and piss."

In *The Bachelor of Salamanca,* Le Sage has a hero whose misfortunes would lead us to suspect that he had been reading of some of the doings of the Kamtchatkan god Kutka, who, among the numerous pranks played upon him by his enemies, the mice, suffered the ignominy of having "a bag made of fish-skin attached to his *orificium ani* while he lay sound asleep. On his way home Kutka desired to relieve nature, but was much surprised on leaving, at the insignificant deposit notwithstanding that he had freed himself of so great a burden. Steller concludes, "Surprised at his cleanliness, he narrated the circumstances to Clacy (his wife), who soon discovered the true state of affairs, and pulling off Kutka's pantaloons, detached the heavily laden bag with great laughter."

According to *Native Tribes of South Australia*, the tribes of the Narinyeri of Encounter Bay have a legend that difference in language was caused when certain of their ancestors "ate the contents of the intestines of the goddess Wurruri."

The Encounter Bay people have another myth, which might have been attributed by Dean Swift to the Yahoos, so foul an origin does it attribute to mankind. It says, "Mingarope having retired upon a natural occasion was highly pleased with the red color of her excrement, which she began to mould into the form of a man, and tickling it, it showed signs of life and began to laugh."

According to Smyth's *Aborigines of Victoria*, the Creation Myth of the Australians relates that the god "Bund-jil created the ocean by urinating for many days upon the orb of the earth." The natives say that the god being angry *bullarto bulgo* upon the earth. *Bullarto bulgo* indicates a great flow of urine. There was another god, named Nurunduri, of whom the story is told that he once made water in a certain spot, "from which circumstance the place is called *Kain-jamin* (to make water.)"

Andrew Lang states in *Myth, Ritual, and Religion*: "In other myths in the Brahmanas, Prajapati creates man from his body, or rather the fluid of his body becomes a tortoise, the tortoise becomes a man, etc."

He also adds, "Moffatt is astonished at the South African notion that the sea was accidentally created by a girl." Perhaps this tale belongs to our series of myths.

In the cosmogonical myths of the islanders of Kadiack, it is related by Lisiansky in *Voyage Round the World* that the first woman, "by making water, produced seas."

Franz Boas says, "The Central Eskimo believe that rain is the urine of a deity."

Ireland has been called the "Urinal of the Planets" from the constant and copious rains which visit it.

In the fourteenth-century farce of *Le Muynier,* the miller has absorbed some of the popular ideas of his day, professed by certain philosophers of the time. He believes that, at the moment of death, the soul of a man escapes by the anus, and warns the priest to absolve him from his sins, saying: "My belly is quite determined. Alas! I don't know what I should do. Go away!"

The priest answers: "But think of your soul's grace!"

Then the miller remarks: "Go away, for I am about to besmirch myself."

The wife and the priest pull the sick man to the edge of the bed and place him in such a position that if the doctrine of soul-departure via the anus be true, they may witness the miller's final performance. The phenomenon of rectal flatulence is now observed, when suddenly, to the consternation of the wife and priest, a demon appears and, placing a sack over the dying miller's anus, catches the rectal gas and flies off in sulphurous vapor.

25.

URINOSCOPY,

or

DIAGNOSIS

by

URINE

HE EXAMINATION OF THE URINE AND FECES OF the sick seems to have obtained in all parts of the world, and among all sorts of people; but in the earlier stages of human progress it was complicated with ideas of divination and forecast, which would make it a religious observance.

According to Pliny, the health of a patient was shown by the condition of his urine.

In the index to the works of Avicenna there are two hundred and seventy-five references to the appearance, etc., of the urine of the sick.

From an examination of the feces and urine of the patient to determine his present state of health, and if possible to make a prognosis of his future condition, was, in the minds of ignorant or half-educated men, merely the first step in the direction of determining the future of the commonwealth by an inspection of the viscera and the excrement of the victims whose food smoked upon its altars. The Romans were addicted to this mode of divination, which Schurig incorrectly styles "Anthropomancy." He relates that Heliogabalus was especially fond of this, and, indeed, he credits that voluptuary with its introduction, and expresses his gratification that he met his desserts in being killed in a privy and left to die in ordure. The Saxons also were given to this method of consulting the future.

According to W. W. Rockhill, Thibetan doctors examine the urine of the patient, then churn it and listen to the noise made by the bubbles.

The people of Europe did not restrict their examinations to the egestae of human beings; they were equally careful to scrutinize every day the droppings of the hounds, hawks, and other animals used in the chase.

In the farce of *Master Pathelin* (A.D. 1480), the hero, "in his ravings abuses the doctors for not understanding his urine. Charlatans especially exploited in this field of medicine, practising it illegally in the country under the name of 'water-jugglers' and 'water-judges.' Such men still practise in Normandy and in certain northern provinces of France."

Montaigne tells the story of a gentleman who always kept for seven or eight days his excrements, in different basins, in order to talk about and show them.

Speaking of melancholy people, Burton says, "Their urine is most part pale and low-colored, '*urina pauca, acris, biliosa,*' and not much in quantity. Their melancholy excrements, in some very much, in others little."

26.

ORDURE
and
URINE
in
MEDICINE

HE ADMINISTRATION OF URINE AS A CURATIVE opens the door to a flood of thought. In the opinion of the author, this part of the investigation should have been assumed by a student possessed of a preliminary training in medicine, and it was not until urged on by friendly correspondents that he concluded, upon resuming his labors, to augment these references by citations from the more prominent writers of ancient and modern times, who have demonstrated the importance of the subject by devoting to its consideration not passing sentences and scant allusions, but pregnant chapters and bulky volumes.

Extracts from the Writings of Dioscorides. Dioscorides lived in the latter years of the first and the opening ones of the second century of the Christian era. He devotes a chapter to the medicinal values of different ordures.

The fresh dung of domestic cattle was considered good for inflamed wounds, for pains at the extremity of the spine, and, when made into a plaster with oil, it dissolved glandular and scrofulous swellings and tumors. The dung of bulls was a remedy for falling of the womb. When drunk with wine, it was frequently given as a remedy in epilepsy. It was used also in the cure of suppressed menstruation and to expel the foetus in retarded delivery as well as for the alleviation of gout in the feet.

Dried goat-dung, drunk in wine, checked hemorrhages, as did that of asses and horses.

Dove and poultry dung were given to break up old sores and scrofulous swellings.

Hen-dung was believed to be a specific against the effects of poisonous mushrooms. It was drunk in wine. Hen-dung, especially that laid during the dog-days, was good for dysentery.

Stork-dung was another remedy for epilepsy; it was also to be drunk in wine.

Vulture-dung expelled the foetus.

Crocodile-excrement was in high repute as a cosmetic. Purchasers were warned that it was frequently adulterated with the excrement of starlings fed on rice.

The urine of the patient himself should be drunk in cases of serpent bites, poisons from drugs, bites of scorpions, mad dogs, etc.

Bull's urine was given for the cure of ulcerated ears.

Goat urine expelled stone from the bladder. It was likewise beneficial in dropsy, if drunk daily.

Asses' urine cured mania.

★   ★   ★

Sextus Placitus. The author is supposed to have lived in the beginning of the fourth century after Christ. The edition of his work, *De Medicamentis ex Animalibus*, was printed in Lyons, in 1537.

Goat-urine was given as a drink to dropsical patients. This urine was also drunk by women to relieve suppression of the menses. For ear troubles goat-urine was applied as a lotion.

For inflammation of the joints, goat-dung was dried and applied as a fine powder. For colic, a fomentation of hot goat-dung was applied to the abdomen; for serpent bites it was applied as a plaster, and also drunk in some convenient liquor. For tumors goat-dung was to be applied externally.

For burns, whether by water or fire, burnt cow-dung was to be sprinkled on.

For all kinds of tumors, as well as for every kind of headache, the dung of elephants was applied externally. He also recommends the use of horse-dung externally in the treatment of earache, and for retention of the menses internally.

Cat-dung was used in the eradication of dandruff and of scald in the head.

Vulture-dung, mixed with the white dung of dog, cured dropsy and palsy, especially if from a vulture which had lived on human flesh; to be taken internally.

The urine of a virgin boy or girl was an invaluable application for affections of the eyes; also for stings of bees, wasps, and other insects. As a cure for elephantiasis, the urine of boys was to be drunk freely.

The crust from human urine was useful in burns and in bites of mad dogs. For cancers man's ordure was burnt and sprinkled over the sore places.

Hawk-dung, boiled in oil, made an excellent application for sore eyes. Crow-dung was given to children to cure coughs.

Dove-dung was applied externally to tumors.

Saxon Leechdoms. In *Saxon Leechdoms* is arranged the medical lore of the early centuries of the Saxon occupancy and conquest of England.

"Alexander of Tralles (A.D. 550) guarantees, of his own experience and the approval of almost all the best doctors, dung of a wolf with bits of bone in it" for colic.

Swine dung was applied to warts.

"For the bite of any serpent, melt goat's grease and her turd and wax, and mingle together; work it up, so that a man may swallow it whole."

"For thigh pains, for sore joints, for cancer, against swellings, tugging of sinews, carbuncle, smear with goat's dung."

"For every sore, let one drink bull's urine in hot water; soon it healeth. For a breach or fracture, lay bull's dung warm on the breach. For waters burning or fires, burn bull's dung and shed thereon." The word "shed" as here employed means to urinate, apparently.

"Against shoulder pains, mingle a tord of an old swine."

For a leper, boil in urine hornbeam, elder, and other barks and roots.

"A wound salve for lung diseases"–of this the dung of goose was an important ingredient.

"A salve for every wound. Collect cow-dung, cow-stale, work up a large kettle full into a batter, as a man worketh soap, then take apple-tree rind" and other rinds mentioned and make a lotion.

"For a horse's leprosy, take piss, heat it with stones, wash the horse with the piss so hot."

"Against cancer, take a man's dung, dry it thoroughly, rub to dust, apply it. If with this thou were not able to cure him, thou mayst never do it by any means."

"Against a penetrating worm, smear with thy spittle and bathe with hot cow-stale."

"Against a warty eruption, warm and apply the sharn or dung of a calf or of an old ox."

"An asses tord was recommended to be applied to weak eyes."

Human Ordure. Daniel Beckherius cites a case in *Medicus Microcosmus* where its use for three days cured a man of yellow jaundice. Dried, powdered, and drunk in wine, it cured febrile paroxysms. It was recommended to be that of a boy fed for some time on bread and beans.

To smell human ordure in the morning, fasting, protected from plague, according to Beckherius.

The ponderous tomes of Michael Etmuller contain all that was known or believed in on this subject at the time of their publication, A.D. 1690. He gives reasons for the employment of each excrement, solid and liquid, human or animal, which need not be detailed at this moment.

A urine bath was good for gout in the feet. A drink of one's own urine was highly praised as a preservative from the plague.

Then there was a *"spiritus urinae per putrefactionem."* To make this, the urine of a boy twelve years old, who had been drinking wine, was placed in a receptacle, surrounded by horse-dung for forty days, allowed to putrefy, then decanted upon human ordure, and distilled in an alembic, etc. There were other methods for making this also, but this one will suffice. The resulting fluid was looked upon as a great "anodyne" for all sorts of pains, and given both internally and externally, as well as in scurvy, hypochondria, cachexy, yellow and black jaundice, calculi of the kidneys and bladder, epilepsy, and mania.

Etmuller tells the same story we have already had from so many other sources, in regard to the medicinal properties ascribed to human ordure. It was looked upon as a valuable remedy, applied as a poultice for all inflammations and suppurations, carbuncles and pest buboes, administered for the cure of bites of serpents, and all venomous animals. It should be taken raw, dried, or in drink. It was the only specific against the bites of the serpents of India, especially the *napellus*, whose bite kills in four hours unless the patient adopts this method of cure. It was considered a specific against the plague, and of great use in effecting "magico-magnetic" or "sympathetic or transplantation" cures. It was also in high repute for baffling the efforts of witches.

Water distilled from ordure was good for sore eyes, especially if the man whose ordure was used had been fed only on bread and wine. This was administered internally for dropsy, calculus, epilepsy, bites of mad dogs, carbuncles, etc."

Christian Franz Paullini's *Filth Pharmacy* (Frankfurt, 1696) is better known than any of the works cited, confining itself almost exclusively to a recapitulation of diseases, with the appropriate excrementitious curative opposite each.

A remedy for epilepsy was to take the excrements of a fine, healthy youth, dry them, and extract the oil by means of heat. Rectify this oil and take inwardly.

Earache or ringing in the ear, or abscesses. Apply the urine of young boys mixed with honey, or apply fresh human urine.

Toothache. Apply a poultice of human excrement, mixed with camomile-flowers, to the cheek.

Dropsy of the head. Take boy's urine internally.

Consumption. The patient's ordure, internally; his own or a boy's urine, or mice-dung, internally.

Another remedy for consumption was to let the patient drink a mixture of his own urine beaten up with fresh egg. Repeat for several successive mornings. Also, let him eat his own excrement.

Cancer of the breast. The patient's own ordure internally, with external applications of the dung of geese, cows, goats, or rabbits.

Dysentery. The patient's own ordure or that of a boy, internally; human urine, internally; or the excreta of dogs, horses, hogs, crows, rabbits, donkeys, mules, or elephants, internally.

Syphillis and venereal diseases. Human urine, internally, also externally; and the excreta of horse and dogs, externally.

Bloody flux. Human excrements dried, taken internally, are of great benefit.

Schurig's Ideas Regarding the Use in Medicine of the Egestae of Animals. Martin Schurig's *Chylologia* published in Dresden in 1725 contains citations from nearly seven hundred authorities. Schurig devotes the fourteenth chapter of his work to a treatise "De Stercoribus Brutorum." It is unnecessary to enter much into detail upon this point. It will be sufficient to give only a small number of the recipes, with notes upon the manner of administering, and, where possible, the opinions expressed in regard to their efficacy.

Asses' dung was considered by Schurig to be an especially good remedy in all diseases of hemorrhage; but it had to be collected in the month of May. It was to be taken in doses of one or more drams, or only the juice squeezed from it into some medicinal water. Dried in the sun, or in a warm place, it was good for bleeding at the nose. It was regarded as an infallible remedy for restraining an excessive menstrual flow. This dung was also in great vogue in all cases of uterine inflammation, applied locally as a plaster. It was administered both internally and externally for gout of the feet, and used as a component of a plaster for dropsy. It was given internally for colic. Collected in the month of May, it was administered internally to dissolve calculi.

Schurig devotes considerable space to the dung of dogs, called by some "Flowers of Melampius," and by other the "more honest name of *album Graecum*." *Album Graecum* was considered best when obtained from "white" dogs, as they were supposed to have the soundest constitutions. This was especially the case in the treatment of epilepsy. Here we have a very decided trace of "Color Symbolism." *Album Graecum* was taken, preferentially, from dogs which, for at least three days previously, had been nourished on hard bones, with the least possible amount of water to drink. Such dung was hard, white, and of faint odor. Some of the prescriptions call for the dung of a fasting dog, "*stercum canis per jejunium emaciati.*"

A rustic remedy which seems to have had a wide dissemination, for the alleviation of the cramp-colic, was composed of the juice expressed from horse-dung, mixed with warm beer, taken internally, while at the same time there was applied to the region of the umbilicus a plaster of warm horse-dung and hot ashes. Such a plaster was employed in the cure of pleurisy among the English. In the same disease a mixture of warm horse-dung and beer was taken both internally and externally.

Lion-dung exerted its potency in cases of difficult labor, and it was the panacea against epilepsy and apoplexy. One of the Grand Dukes of Austria was cured of epilepsy by its use. Preference was given to the excrement of a female lion, except where she had just brought forth young. An anti-epileptic remedy of great repute was composed of burnt crow's nest, burnt tortoise, burnt human skulls, linden-tree bark, and lion-dung, made into an infusion by long digestion in spirits of wine.

Schurig recommends the use of mouse-dung, both internally and externally, for various disorders, for constipation in children, for scald head, and dandruff, in which cases it was applied as an ointment, for the elimination of calculi in kidneys and bladder, for all swellings in the fundament, piles, warts, tumors *in ano*, hemorrhages of the lungs, for the suppression of the menses, and even to excite the growth of the beard. When taken internally, it was administered in broth, milk, or panada; externally, it was made into a plaster with butter and such ingredients. It was at times mixed with the dung of sparrows.

★   ★   ★

Ordure and Urine in Folk-Medicine. Excrementitious remedies are still to be met with in the folk-medicine of various countries. The extracts to be now given will show that folk-medicine still retains a hold upon medicaments the use of which is generally believed to have passed away with the centuries.

Captain Henri Jouan of the French Navy writes in a personal letter from Cherbourg, France: "I never had an opportunity of seeing the following deed, but it was many times asserted to me by serious persons. In our province, Brittany, when somebody in the peasantry has a cheek swollen by the effects of toothache, a very good remedy is to apply upon the swollen cheek, as a poultice, freshly expelled cow-dung, and even human dung, just expelled and still smoking, which is considered as much more efficient."

Swine's dung was used as a remedy for dysentery in Ireland. This is alluded to in terms of high approval by Borlase as quoted by Southey in the *Commonplace Book.*

In a personal letter dated from April 16, 1888, Professor S. B. Evans reports: "I am impressed to tell you of a custom that prevailed to some extent among the people of Iowa. This was the use of sheep-dung for measles. The dung was made into what the old women denominated 'tea,' and was familiarly known as 'sheep-nanny tea.' It was believed to be singularly efficacious in bringing out the eruption. The mixture was sweetened with sugar, and thus disguised was given to children. This practice was kept up among certain classes until about twenty years ago; I have not heard of it, at least in recent years. I can trace the custom through the origin of the families in which it was practised here to Indiana and North Carolina."

This use of sheep-dung in the treatment of measles must be very ancient and widespread. Surgeon Washington Matthews notes its existence among the Navajoes, who learned it from the Spaniards.

Lye-tea, made of human urine and lime-water, was used for colds by the "old people" in the rural parts of Central New York.

Mr. Chrisfield of the Library of Congress in Washington, D.C. states that urine was a remedy for earache among people on the Eastern Shore of Maryland and Virginia.

Mrs. Fanny D. Bergen of Cambridge, Massachusetts has for some years devoted time and intelligent study to the acquisition of data bearing upon the superstitions connected with the human saliva. While making this valuable and curious collection she has also been fortunate enough to encounter much relating to kindred superstitions, and has very generously placed at the disposal of the author of this volume all that related to the employment of human and animal egestae.

Urine a cure for chapped hands, on Deer Isle.

Boys urinate on their legs to prevent cramp. This practice was common in eastern Maine twenty or thirty years ago.

Water standing in the depressions of cow-dung was formerly recommended as a certain cure for pulmonary consumption, in New York.

A poultice of fresh, warm cow-dung cured a man of rheumatism in New York.

Cow-manure was used for swelled breasts in County Cork, Ireland.

The white, limy part of hen-manure was used for canker-sores in the mouth in Abingdon, Illinois.

Professor E. N. Horsford of Harvard University says the following in a personal letter: "The presence of ammonia in the secretions (whose power of neutralizing acids may have been accidentally discovered) may have had something to do with the repute of the excretions of the kidneys. I remember to have been told as a little boy of the virtues of urine as a relief to chapped hands, also as a counter-irritant for inflamed eyes. In the former case the ammonia would soften as an alkali; in the latter, the salts present would act to reduce congestion, like common salt, by endosmosis."

Cosmetics. Pigeon's dung was applied externally for all spots and blemishes on the face. "Brand Marks" (stigmata) were removed by using pigeon's dung diluted in vinegar. Crocodile-dung, or *crocodilea*, removed blemishes from the face. It also removed freckles.

Pliny relates, "An application of bull-dung, they say, will impart a rosy tint to the cheeks, and not even *crocodilea* is better for the purpose."

Galen alludes to the extensive use as a cosmetic, by the Greek and Roman ladies, of the dung of the crocodile; in the same manner, the dung of starlings that had been fed on rice alone was employed.

According to Avicenna, dog-urine was prescribed to restore the color of the hair.

The ordure of small lizards was also used to smooth out the wrinkles from the faces of old women.

Fox-dung and the dung of sparrows and starlings were in use for softening the hands. Arabian women use as a cosmetic a mixture of saffron and chicken-dung. Cow-dung is sometimes as aromatic as musk. It used to be employed to restore the odor to old and faded musk, or to hang the latter in a privy, where it would re-acquire its former strength; but would not retain it long.

To improve the complexion, Paullini recommended a water distilled from human excrements; also the worms that grow therein distilled to a water.

The cosmetic of country wenches is their own urine. Human excrements have peculiar salts more strengthening and useful than soap. A young girl improved her complexion wonderfully by washing her face in cow-dung and drinking her brother's urine fresh and warm, while fasting.

For the eradication of freckles, Paullini also recommended the external application of the excrement of donkeys, dogs, chickens, crocodiles, foxes, or pigeons.

Professor Patrice de Janon states that the ladies of his native place in Cartagena, Columbia, to his personal knowledge, were in the habit of using their own urine as a face lotion, and to beautify and soften the skin.

Goose-dung is in repute in the State of Indiana for removing pimples, according to Mrs. Bergen.

Mr. Sylvester Baxter says that young women in Massachusetts, at least until very recently, have employed human urine as a wash for the preservation of the complexion.

27.

WITCHCRAFT, SORCERY, CHARMS, SPELLS, INCANTATIONS, MAGIC

 XACTLY WHERE THE SCIENCE OF MEDICINE ended and the science of witchcraft began, there is no means of knowing. Like Astrology and Astronomy, they were twin sisters, issuing from the same womb, and travelling amicably hand in hand for many years down the trail of civilization's development. Long after medicine had won for herself a proud position in the world of thought and felt compelled through shame to repudiate her less-favored comrade in public, the strictest and closest relations were maintained in the seclusion of private life.

Human and animal filth are mentioned in nearly every treatise upon witchcraft, under three different heads:

Firstly, as the means by which the sorcery is accomplished.

Secondly, as the antidote by which such machinations are frustrated.

Thirdly, as the means of detecting the witch's personality.

Muhongo, a boy from Angola, said in a personal interview:

"Sorcerers try to procure some of a man's excrement, and put it in his food in order to kill him." Muhongo also said that to "add one's urine, even unintentionally, to the food of another bewitches that other, and does him grievous harm."

Johannes Frommann writes in *Tractatus de Fascinatione* that human ordure, menses, and semen were mixed in the food of the person to be bewitched. On another page, this list is increased to read that human ordure, urine, blood, hair, nails, bones, skulls, and the moss growing on the last-named, as well as animal excrement, were among the materials employed in witchcraft.

Adam Krusenstern reports in *Voyage Round the World*: "He who wishes to revenge himself by witchcraft endeavors to procure either the saliva, urine, or excrements of his enemy, and after mixing them with a powder, and putting them into a bag woven in a particular form, he buries them."

John Matthews reports from his experience with the aborigines of Australia: "If the death of any obnoxious person is desired to be procured by sorcery, the malevolent native secures a portion of his enemy's hair, refuse of food, or excrement. These substances are carried in a bag specially reserved for the artillery of witchcraft, a little wallet which is slung over the shoulders. The refuse of food is subjected to special treatment, part of which is scorching and melting before a fire. But, in the case of excrement, my information is to the effect that it is just allowed to moulder away, and as it decays the health and strength of the enemy is supposed to decline contemporaneously. Excrement is thus employed in the south of Queensland."

According to Paullini, human ordure and urine were burned

with live coals as a potent charm. The person whose excreta had been burned would suffer terrible pains in the rectum. But this could be used in two ways, for love as well as hatred could be induced by this means between married people and between old friends.

Etmuller says that a bone from the leg or thigh of a man who had died a violent death, emptied of its marrow, and then filled with human ordure, closed up with wax, and placed in boiling water, compelled the unfortunate ejector of the excrement to evacuate just as long as the bone was kept in the water, and it could even be so used that he would be compelled to defile his bed every night.

"In order to produce a flux in the belly, it was only necessary to put a patient's excrement into a human bone, and throw it into a stream of water." The above is quoted from the medical writings of Peter of Spain, who was archbishop, and afterwards Pope, under the name of John XXI.

Schurig names many authors to show that in cases of "incivility," such as the placing of excrement at the door of one's neighbor, the person offended had a sure remedy in his own hands. He was to take some of the excrement of the offending party, mix it with live coals or hot ashes, and throw it out in the street; or he could burn pepper and wine together, with such fecal matter; or he could heat an iron to white heat, insert it in the excrement, and as fast as it cooled, repeat the operation. As often as this was done, so often would the guilty one suffer pains in the anus. Other remedies were, to mix spirits of wine and salt together, sprinkle upon the offensive matter, then place a red-hot iron above it, and confer the same pains, which would not leave the offending person's anus during the whole of that day, unless he cured himself with new milk. Or small peas could be heated in a frying-pan, and then thrown out with fresh excrement. As many as there were peas, so many would be the pains endured by the delinquent.

That the Eskimo believed in the power of human ordure to baffle witchcraft would seem to be intimated in the following from Franz Boas's "The Central Eskimo": "Though the *Angekok* understood the schemes of the old hag, he followed her, and sat down with her. She feigned to be very glad to see him and gave him a dishful of soup, which he began to eat. But by the help of his *tornag* (that is, the magical influence which aided him) the food fell right through him into a vessel which he had put between his feet on the floor of the hut. This he gave to the old witch, and compelled her to eat it. She died as soon as she had brought the first spoonful to her mouth."

The Eskimo living near Point Barrow have a yearly ceremony for driving out an evil spirit which they call Tuna. The "Report of the International Polar Expedition to Point Barrow" reports that among the ceremonies incident to the occasion is this. One of the performers "brought a vessel of urine and flung it on the fire."

To frustrate the effects of witchcraft, Dr. Rosinus Lentilius recommended that the patient take a quantity of his own ordure, the size of a filbert, and drink it in oil. According to Paullini, the antidotes were to take human ordure both internally and externally, and human urine externally. Schurig, for the same purpose, recommended human urine and ordure, but both to be taken internally, mixed with hyoscyamine.

Schurig relates that the countrywomen in Germany, if after milking their cows for a long time they were unable to bring the proper quantity of butter, suspected that they were under the spell of a witch. To undo this spell it was only necessary to mix some fresh milk with human ordure and throw the mixture down the privy. Schurig also prescribed hen and dove dung for the cure of the bewitched.

Beckherius highly extolled human ordure for the same purpose. He tells the story of the Lapland witches being able to hold a ship in its course, except when the inner seams of the vessel had been calked with the ordure of a virgin.

Reginald Scot writes in *Discoverie of Witchcraft*: "To unbewitch the bewitched, you must spit into the pisse-pot where you have made water."

According to Franz Boas, "the Shamans of the Thlinkeets of Alaska keep their urine until its smell is so strong that the spirits cannot endure it."

The Thlinkeet of the northwest coast of America believe that a drowned man can be restored to life by cutting the skin and applying a medicine made of certain roots infused in the urine of a child, who has been kept for three moons. Drowned men, according to their medicine-men, are turned into otters.

Brand's *Popular Antiquities* states: "It was a supposed remedy against witchcraft to put some of the bewitched person's water, with a quantity of pins, needles, and nails, into a bottle, cork them up, and set them before the fire, in order to confine the spirit. But this sometimes did not prove sufficient, as it would often force the cork out with a loud noise, like that of a pistol, and cast the contents to a considerable height."

Paullini says, "To ascertain if one be bewitched, take his urine and boil it in a new unused pot. If it foam up, he is not bewitched; if not, it is uncertain. Or, take clean ashes, put them in a new pot, let the patient urinate thereon. Tie up the pot, and let it stand in the sun; then break the ashes apart. If this person be bewitched, hairs will be found therein."

According to Beckherius, to determine whether a woman be pregnant of a boy or a girl, make two small holes in the ground. In one, put wheat; in the other, barley. Let her urinate on both. If the wheat sprout first, she will have a boy; if the barley, a girl. To determine whether a man had been attacked by leprosy (elephantiasis), the ashes of burnt lead were thrown into his urine. If they fell to the bottom, he was well; if they floated on top, he was in danger.

To determine whether a sick man was to die during the current month, some of his urine was shaken up in a glass vessel until it foamed. Then the observer took some of his own earwax and placed it in the foam. If it separated, the man was to recover; if not, not.

Brand says in his article on "Nose and Mouth Omens": "Poor Robin, in his *Almanac* for 1695, ridicules the following indelicate fooleries then in use, which must surely have been either of Dutch or Flemish extraction. 'They who when they make water go streaking the walls with their urine, as if they were planning some antic figures or making some curious delineations, or shall piss in the dust, making I know not what scattering angles and circles, or some chink in the wall, or a little hole in the ground, are to be brought in, after two or three admonitions, as incurable fools.' This was possibly a survival from some old method of divining."

In the valuable compilation of superstitious practices interdicted by Roman Catholic councils (*Traité des Superstitions*), Jean Baptiste Thiers includes the persons who bathe their hands with urine in the morning to avert witchcraft or nullify its effect. He says, too, that Saint Lucy was reputed to be a witch, for which reason the Roman judge, Paschasius, sprinkled her with urine at her trial.

There is on record the confession of a young French witch, Jeanne Bosdean, at Bordeaux in 1594, wherein is described a witches' mass at which the devil appeared in the disguise of a black buck with a candle between his horns. When holy water was needed, the buck urinated in a hole in the ground and the officiating witch aspersed it upon the congregation with a black sprinkler. Jeanne Bosdean adhered to her story even when in the flames.

According to Reginald Scot, one of the ceremonies of the initiation of the neophytes into witchcraft was "kissing the devil's bare buttocks." Pope Gregory IX, in a letter addressed to several German bishops in 1234, describes the initiation of sorcerers as follows: The novices, on being introduced into the assembly, "see a toad of enormous size. Some kiss its mouth, others its rear." Next, "a black cat is presented. The novice kisses the rear anatomy of the cat, after which he salutes in a similar manner those who preside at the feast, and others worthy of the honor." Again, in Dr. Dupouy's *Medicine in the Middle Ages,* "At witches' reunions, the possessed kissed the devil's rear, kissing it goat fashion, in a butting attitude."

In *Sorcery and Magic,* Thomas Wright calls attention to the fact that at the meetings of witches, "at times, every article of luxury was placed before them, and they feasted in the most sumptuous manner. Often, however, the meats served on the table were nothing but toads and rats, and other articles of a revolting nature. In general they had no salts, and but seldom bread." After these feasts came "wild and uproarious dancing and revelry. Their backs, instead of their faces, were turned inwards. It may be observed, as a curious circumstance, that the modern waltz is first traced among the meetings of the witches and their imps. The songs were generally obscene or vulgar, or ridiculous."

The initiates in witchcraft may have been compelled to adopt loathsome foods as a test of the sincerity of their purposes, or they may have taken them to induce an intoxication such as that of the Zuñis of New Mexico and the wild tribes of Siberia. There is still another hypothesis to be considered before relinquishing this topic. The best food, we know, was always offered to the deities of the ruling sect, and the use of any of the appurtenants of the rites of the ruling religion in the ceremonial of a superseded cult was looked upon as the veriest sacrilege and blasphemy. For example, the use of holy water at the witches' sabbath was considered a worse crime than that of being a witch. Therefore we may conclude that, as the votaries of the superseded religion did not dare to employ the best, they necessarily had to fall back upon inferior material out of which to construct their oblations. And, as they assembled generally in mountain recesses, in caves, etc., where nothing better could be had, they offered themselves in sacrifice—that is, they recurred to the old practices of human sacrifice, if indeed they had ever abandoned them, and gave the pledges of their hair, saliva, urine, and egestae.

The presents which the devil gave to witches all turned into filth the next morning. For a specimen of the filthy in literature, read the dream of Zador of Vera Cruz, who wished to sell his soul to the devil in *The Bachelor of Salamanca* (Paris, 1847) by Le Sage.

The best explanation of the above story—which represents Zador as making a compact with his satanic majesty whereby in exchange for Zador's soul the devil discloses a gold mine in a graveyard, from which the poor dupe extracts enough for his present needs, and then marks the locality by an ingenious method, only to be awakened by his angry wife to the mortifying consciousness that he has defiled his own bed—is that it reflects the current opinion of the Spaniards of Le Sage's era in regard to the transmutability of the gifts received from the evil one.

Pliny says, "The adepts in magic expressly forbid a person, when about to make water, to uncover the body in the face of the sun or moon, or to sprinkle with his urine the shadow of any object whatsoever. Hesiod gives a precept recommending persons to make water against an object standing full before them, that no divinity may be offended by their nakedness being uncovered. Osthanes maintains that every one who drops some urine upon his foot in the morning will be proof against all noxious medicaments."

The adepts in the magical art also believed that "it is improper to spit into the sea, or to profane that element by any other of the evacuations that are inseparable from the infirmities of nature."

Some of these ideas would appear to have crossed the Atlantic. In the United States, a generation or less ago, boys were wont to urinate "criss-cross" for good luck and were careful not to let any of their urine fall on their own shadows.

The old home of the Cheyennes of Dakota was in the Black Hills; and there the Sioux believed that the Cheyennes were invincible, because their medicine-men could make everything out of buffalo manure.

In *Across Africa,* Charles Cameron, describing the dance of a medicine-man in the village of Kwinhata, near the head of the Congo, and the humble deference shown to these Mganga by the women, says of one of the women: "She soon went away quite happy, the chief Mganga having honored her by spitting in her face and giving her a ball of beastliness as a charm. This she hastened to place in safety in her hut."

According to Georg Schweinfurth's *Heart of Africa,* the bed chamber of Munza, King of the Mombottoes, was "painted with many geometrical designs with the white from dog's dung (*album Graecum*)." It is quite safe to assert that these "geometrical designs" were "magical."

James Mooney's "Medical Mythology of Ireland" leaves no uncertainty in regard to the mystic powers ascribed by the Celtic peasantry to both urine and ordure. Mooney relates an instance of the abduction of an Irishwoman by fairies. She managed to impart to her husband the knowledge of the means by which her rescue could be accomplished: "He must be ready with some urine and some chicken-dung, which he must throw upon her, and then seize her. Soon he heard the fairies approaching, and when the noise came in front of him he threw the dung and urine in the direction of the sound, and saw his wife fall from her horse." The Irish peasantry firmly believe in the power of the fairies to carry off their children. To effect a restoration, "a wise woman" is summoned, whose method is to "heat the shovel in the fireplace, place the changeling upon it, and put it out upon the dunghill." Mooney concludes, "Fire, iron, and dung, the three great safe-guards against the influence of fairies and the infernal spirits."

Dung is carried about the person as part of the contents of am-ulets; and children suffering from convulsions are, as a last resort, bathed from head to foot in urine, to rescue them from the clutches of their fairy persecutors.

28.

CURES

by

TRANSPLANTATION

HE MOST CURIOUS METHOD OF ALLEVIATING physical and mental disorders was that termed by various writers: "Cures by Transplantation," by "Translation," by "Sympathy," and by "Magnetic Transference." Frommann opens the way to a clearer understanding of the principles upon which these cures depended in *Tractatus de Fascinatione*. He states that that not all diseases were thus curable; only those which in themselves were "movable."

Frommann devotes a long chapter to cures by "transplantation." He cites from Pliny the method of curing a bad cough by spitting into the mouth of a toad, and also gives another in which the urine of the patient made into a dough with flour, was given to a dog or hog.

Frommann believed with Von Helmont that there was nothing superstitious about such cures, because there were no rites and no incantations used. But later on, he mentions having heard a woman (who was trying one of these cures by rolling some of her son's hair in wax and burying the wax ball in an incision in an apple-tree) recite certain words, which she declined to repeat for him when asked; hence, he was in some doubt about her particular case. He quotes the English Count of Digby as stating that he knew of a nurse who carelessly allowed some of a baby's excrement to be burned up in a fire. The result was the child suffered terribly from excoriation of the fundament. The way in which a cure was effected in this case was the "sympathetic" one of placing the baby's excrements for three days in a basin filled with cold water, and exposing in a cold place.

Frommann quotes Ratray as saying from his own observation that there was a "sympathy" between the patient's urine when enclosed in a glass vial and the condition of the patient himself–a sort of "barometrical" sympathy, as we would term it. At an earlier period of culture, the urine would have been placed in the horn of a goat or in the bladder of a hog.

The first excrement of a man sick with dysentery was mixed with salt as a "magnetic" cure. To this, some people added the powder of eel-skins. Yellow jaundice patients urinated upon clean linen sheets. If they succeeded in dyeing them yellow they would recover soon; if not, not. Roots wet with the patient's urine were burned as a cure for the yellow jaundice.

For the cure of jaundice, Hoffman's "Folk Medicine of the Pennsylvania Germans" advises the following: "Hollow out a carrot, fill it with the patient's urine, and hang it, by means of a string, in the fireplace. As the urine is evaporated, and the carrot becomes shrivelled, the disease will leave the patient. In this, there is an evident belief in the connection between the properties and color of the carrot and the yellow skin of the patient having jaundice. To this class may belong the belief respecting the use of a band of red flannel for diphtheria, and yellow or amber beads for purulent discharges from the ears."

Thomas Pettigrew's *Medical Superstitions* states: "Seven or nine—it must be an odd number—cakes, made of the newly emitted urine of a patient, with the ashes of ash wood, and buried for some days in a dunghill, will, according to Paracelsus, cure the yellow jaundice."

A patient suffering from yellow jaundice should urinate upon horse-dung while warm. This same remedy seems to have been in vogue in helping women in the expulsion of the placenta. One of the prescriptions given by Schurig states that the horse-dung must be from an animal that was not tired at the time of the evacuation—*"non defatigati."*

According to Etmuller, a "sympathetic" cure by the use of the dung of horses seems to be implied in the case of infants' smallpox, where we find it suspended in beer.

For consumption, Beckherius gives a "sympathetic" cure of boiling an egg in the patient's urine until it hardens, and then burying it in an ant-hill. The same cure was employed in fevers.

Paullini taught that fevers of all kinds could be cured by pouring the patient's urine into a fish pond. "Such of the fish as drink of their water," he says, "will receive the fever, which will leave the sick man."

By the French, urine was considered a certain cure for fever. Such an amount of superstition attached to the panacea that the prescription may well be given in full: "Knead a small loaf with urine voided in the worst stage of his fever by a person having the quaternary ague. Bake the loaf, let it cool, and give it to be eaten by another person. Repeat the same during three different attacks, and the fever will leave the patient and go to the person who has eaten the bread."

Another one cited by Thiers' *Traité des Superstitions* runs in these terms: "Take an egg, boil it hard, and break off the shell. Prick the egg in different places with a needle, steep it in the urine of a person afflicted with fever, and then give it to a man if the patient be a man, to a woman if a woman, and the recipient will acquire the fever, which will abandon the patient."

Sextus Placitus relates that goat-urine was applied to sore eyes, but a more certain cure in grave cases was additionally effected by hanging some of it in a goat's horn for twenty days.

According to Schurig, for the "sympathetic" cure of hernia, the root of the herb "wallwort" was smeared with the ordure of the patient, and then buried in the ground.

To stop hemorrhage "sympathetically," whether from wounds or other injuries, some of the flowing blood was taken and mixed with the ordure of the patient, and the mixture then exposed in a jar to the action of the air.

Hoffman reports in "Folk-Lore of the Pennsylvania Germans": "Blisters on the tongue are caused by telling fibs. When they show no disposition to leave, the following process is adopted. Three small sticks are cut from a tree, each about the length of a finger, and as thick as a pencil. These are inserted in the mouth, and buried in a dung-hill. The next day the operation is repeated, as well as on the third day; after which the three sets of sticks are allowed to remain in the manure, and as they decay, the complaint will disappear."

"Convulsions in a child are sometimes due to the influence of the fairies." In "Medical Mythology of Ireland," James Mooney describes a cure effected by a mother who "picked from the roadside ten small white pebbles, known as 'fairy stones.' On reaching home, she put nine of these stones into a vessel of urine and threw the tenth into the fire. She also put into the vessel some chicken-dung and three sprigs of a plant (probably ivy or garlic) which grew on the roof above the door. She then stripped the child and threw into the fire the shirt and other garments which were worn next the skin. The child was then washed from head to foot, wrapped in a blanket, and put to bed. There were nine hens and a rooster on the rafters above the door. In a short time the child had a violent fit and the nine hens dropped dead upon the floor. The rooster dropped down from his perch, crew three times, and then flew again to the rafters. If the woman had put the tenth stone with the others, he would have dropped dead with the hens. The child was cured."

Mooney remarks upon the above: "This single instance combines in itself a number of important features in connection with the popular mythology—the dung, the urine, the plant above the door, the chickens, the fire and the garment worn next the skin—and introduces also a new element into the popular theory of disease, viz.: the idea of vicarious cure, or rather of vicarious sacrifice. This belief, which is general, is that no one can be cured of a dangerous illness, unless, as the people express it, 'something is left in its place' to suffer the sickness and death.''

A curious method of relieving and eradicating all kinds of colic by "transplantation" is related and described by Schurig. The excrement voided during one of the paroxysms should be buried in an unfrequented spot. The grass growing on the soil where the ordure had been deposited would be eaten by domestic cattle, which would acquire the disease, relieving the sufferer.

Schurig gives the recipe of Johannes Philippus ab Hertodt for the preparation of a "sympathetic" powder, which serves to inform us as to the incoherent ideas of the practitioners of a couple of centuries ago. Freely translated, it reads, "Take of a healthy human mummy, moistened with a little urine. Let it be dried in a place exposed to an east wind, but not to the sun, until it shall be reduced to powder. This is to be mixed with an equal weight of cream of tartar, and the 'sympathetic powder of vitriol,' prepared according to formula, in the dog-days; or of the salt of Hungarian vitriol, heated to whiteness in a furnace. A pinch of this sympathetic powder should be sprinkled upon the feces of the sick person, or upon a cloth dipped in his urine, and then preserved in a cool place.'' Its efficacy was vouched for in the highest terms.

Schurig concludes, "The various modes of application of these remedies are too long for insertion here, but are valuable to the student as showing how deep-seated was the belief in the occult properties of the excreta themselves.''

29.

PHALLIC SUPERSTITIONS

in

FRANCE

and

OTHER PARTS OF EUROPE

 MONG THE PEASANTRY OF IRELAND THERE ARE in use certain prehistoric arrow-heads, believed by them to be fairy darts. According to Mooney's *Medical Mythology of Ireland,* "When an illness is supposed to be due to the influence of the fairies, this 'fairy dart' is put into a tumbler and covered with water, which the patient then drinks, and if the fairies are responsible for his sickness, he at once recovers."

And in like manner—as has already been shown of the sacred character attaching, among the people of the far East, to water, wine, or milk which had been poured over the lingam—the women of France solaced themselves with the hope that children would come to those who drank an infusion containing scrapings from the phalli, existing until the outbreak of the French revolution, at Puy en Velay, in the church of Saint Foutin, in the shrine of Saint Guerlchon, near Bruges, in the shrine of Guignolles, near Brest; and in that of an ancient statue of Priapus, at Antwerp.

30.

The Use

of

Bladders

in

Making

Excrement Sausages

T was believed to be peculiarly necessary that the urine or ordure of those suffering from epilepsy, yellow jaundice, quartan fevers, etc., should be placed in a pig's bladder, and hung up in the chimney, in other words, they were made into excrement sausages.

For the potency of these excrement sausages in rescuing victims from the clutches of witches, from the yellow jaundice, from fevers, and other troubles we have the assurances of such grave and reputable writers as Schurig, Paullini, Etmuller, Frommann, and others of ages past. Meanwhile, William Black's *Folk Medicine* certifies to their use in Staffordshire.

Schurig instances a farmer who by hanging up in his chimney the dung of his neighbor's horses drove them all into a consumption.

According to Paullini, the devil cannot be more completely frustrated than by placing upon some of his works human ordure, or by hanging human ordure in the smoke of the chimney.

In Staffordshire, to cure the yellow jaundice, a bladder was often filled with the urine of the patient and placed near the fire.

In *The Golden Bough,* J. G. Frazer states the following: "In Thuringia a sausage is stuck in the last sheaf at threshing, and thrown with the sheaf on the threshing-floor. It is called the *barrenwurst,* and is eaten by all the threshers. After they have eaten it, a man is encased in pease straw, and thus attired is led through the village."

Attaching to this array of facts the value which properly belongs to each and every one of them, and no more, it seems that the Feast of Fools may be better understood by regarding it as the burlesque and distorted "survival" of a sacred, comitial gathering of the gens or community, in which the excrement sausage served a now completely forgotten purpose in eliminating from the people the baleful curse of witchcraft, epilepsy, jaundice, fevers, and other disorders which would not yield promptly to the simple medicaments of primitive therapeutics.

Index

About the Editor

Dr. Louis Kaplan is a modern cultural historian with a scholarly penchant for the hysterical. Many of his wide-ranging researches have focused on the relations between marginal or subjugated knowledges and humor.

Born in 1960 in the Garden State of New Jersey, he graduated magna cum laude from Harvard College with a A.B. in social studies and later received his master's and doctoral degrees in modern history from the University of Chicago. A version of his dissertation will be published as *Laszlo Moholy-Nagy: Biographical Writings* by Duke University Press in 1995.

In 1989–1990, Kaplan was awarded a Walther Rathenau Postdoctoral Fellowship by the Verbund für Wissenschaftsgeschichte (Alliance for the History of Science) in Berlin to study the exceptional cosmography of the American critic of science and collector of "the data of the damned," Charles Fort (1874–1932). This led to the first German publication about Fort, which was later published in English as *The Damned Universe of Charles Fort* (New York: Autonomedia, 1993).

Dr. Kaplan was awarded a DAAD fellowship to research the scatological humor of the Fluxus art movement in Germany. It was out of these investigations that he became fascinated with John Bourke's ethnological classic, *Scatalogic Rites of All Nations* (1891), and the eccentric science of excremental anthropology. He prepared a revised edition of the German version of the book (1913) that was published as *Das Buch des Unrats* (Frankfurt: Eichborn, 1992).

Kaplan has also published a book (in collaboration) in the field of pop culture and film studies–*Gumby: The Authorized Biography of the World's Favorite Clayboy* (New York: Harmony Books, 1986).

Dr. Kaplan has taught cultural history at the Stanford Study Center in Berlin and the Kansas City Art Institute. At present, he is a Postdoctoral Fellow at the Franz Rosenzweig Research Center for German-Jewish Literature and Cultural History at the Hebrew University of Jerusalem, where he is investigating the genre of the Jewish joke book.